Additional Praise for
Why Can't Banks Be As Easy As Uber?

"An eye-opening book on revolutionary changes in banking. Many ideas on hidden fees in the current industry and a presentation of a completely new, uber-inspired business model."

—Harbir Singh
Vice Dean, Global Initiatives
at the Wharton School

"If you're concerned about the health of your bank account, read this book!"

—Dr. Oz
Host of The Dr. Oz Show

"What a compelling book! The banking revolution that the Sidhu's are proposing is sure to make banking easier—and you happier."

—Tal Ben-Shahar, PhD
New York Times Bestselling Author of *Happier*

*"*Why Can't Banks Be As Easy As Uber? *shines a damning spotlight on the way in which antiquated bank models profit off of their poorest customers."*

—Mary Wisniewski
Fintech Reporter, *American Banker*

"Jay Sidhu is a legend in banking and his daughter Luvleen is emerging as one of fintech's finest innovators. Together they have built one of the most innovative banks in the world, and one that may transform how millions of millennials manage their money.

—Philip Ryan
Senior Editor, Bank Innovation

"For millennials, financial empowerment is a click away as long as that click takes them to a place they trust with their future...BankMobile."

—Joan Kuhl
Founder, Why Millennials Matter

"The story behind the creation of BankMobile is fascinating. It details how the banking system, in general, is broken and why the US needs bank services that are truly customer focused. The technology they put together is far superior to that of the biggest five banks in the U.S."

—David Gerbino
Fintech Consultant

"Why Can't Banks Be As Easy As Uber *is a must read for all Americans.»*

—Steve Zuckerman
Founder and former CEO, Clipper Magazine

"The biggest enemy of young savers and investors can be summed up in one phrase: 'ridiculous fees'. Bankmobile is leading the charge to fundamentally change banking and bring it up to 21st century standards to help the young conveniently save and bank without the handicap of excessive fees"

—Emmanuel Modu
Coauthor of *Teenvestor: The Practical Investment Guide for Teens and Their Parents*

"The most innovative banking service I have come across. This book is a must read."

—Michael Pavone
CEO of Pavone Marketing Agency

Why Can't
BANKS
Be As *Easy* As
UBER?

Why Can't BANKS Be As *Easy* As UBER?

BankMobile and the Real Future of Banking

JAY SIDHU
Co-founder and CEO

LUVLEEN SIDHU
Co-founder and Chief Strategy Officer

ISBN Paperback: 978-1-720-93385-4

Cover Design: Michelle Manley
Interior Design: Ghislain Viau

We dedicate this book to all of our team members who work so hard to make BankMobile one of the most innovative, customer-focused, and fastest-growing banks in the United States.

We especially want to thank Warren Taylor, Kirk Barrett, Dan Armstrong, Jim Collins, and many others who work with passion and purpose to financially empower Americans through BankMobile.

Contents

Boy, Does Banking Ever Need a Makeover!

IF OUR BOOK IS ABOUT BANKING, WHY ARE WE TALKING about Uber?

Because Uber changed everything. And not just the way you hail a cab.

If you've ever used Uber, you know that it makes getting from Point A to Point B laughably simple. Open up the Uber app, tap a couple of prompts, and presto—a clean, comfortable, roadworthy vehicle, driven by an individual who has passed driving and criminal checks, arrives at your door to take you wherever you want to go.

But Uber changed more than just getting around.

It changed the way we think—and not just about the taxi-and-limousine industry.

Remember when people used to say, "If they can put a man on the moon, why can't they . . . ?" And they'd finish the sentence with whatever they thought should be super easy to do but was complicated for no good reason.

Today, people say, "If they can create Uber, and completely change the taxi-and-limousine industry, why can't they change . . . ?"

Everything we do, from the way we travel to the way we shop, from the way we eat to the way we entertain ourselves, has been turned upside down by some Uber-like company or idea. Everything, that is, except banking. Why doesn't your bank behave more like Uber—or Amazon, Airbnb, Facebook, iTunes, Pandora, Fandango, Waze, Seamless, or Netflix, for that matter?

In an era where you can tap an app and buy a book, a plane ticket, a stock, a song, or a vacation rental, banking is stuck in the nineteenth century. That's because banks still spend money on branches (or *stores*, in the parlance of the industry) , in every neighborhood and business district around the country. What they haven't done is create the kind of experience you get on your smartphone from Uber and any of the thousands of other life-enhancing apps. That's because the money that banks could be investing in an Uber-like banking experience is going toward rent, security, and utilities at branch offices instead.

Ever think about the security guards watching over the premises?

You're paying for them.

All the advertising for those banks and all of the other expenses associated with traditional banking—the money for their upkeep—comes out of your pocket. Your paycheck. Your savings.

Need a new bank card? Get ready to spend another hour sitting there, proving to your "customer relationship manager" that you are who you say you are—even though he or she should know that by now.

Need more checks? Hope you aren't in a hurry. They'll take a couple of weeks to arrive.

Need *anything* from a human being? Get ready to waste even more precious minutes of your life waiting, waiting, waiting.

We haven't even gotten to bank fees yet.

Let's get down to brass tacks. Banks don't see you as a customer. They see you as a piñata. It's party time, and they're going to keep whacking you with fee upon fee until there's nothing left in your checking account. No exaggeration. In one case, a fintech CFO opened a checking account in her five-year-old son's name to teach him about the benefits of managing money. The boy's first statement showed a $12 service charge. At that monthly rate, his $100 investment would all but drain away in eight months. And when he got down to his last dollar, the bank would charge him a fee for running out of money.

Better not even try to close the account, because the bank charges for that too!

You cannot make this stuff up.

The dirty little secret of banking is that banks charge you fees — outrageous, unjustifiable, and all too often illegitimate fees — for trying to use your own money the way you want to.

Want to get money from an ATM outside your network? You're going to pay a fee.

Bounce a check? You're going to pay a bigger fee.

Doing just about anything at any bank will trigger a fee.

Each year, banks charge more in overdraft fees alone than what Americans spend on vegetables—about $32 billion. Isn't that outrageous?!

That's how the banks pay for all those shiny branch offices.

That's how bankers pay the salaries of tellers, officers, security guards, cleaning staff, and everyone else.

That's how most banks pay their executive management the big bucks.

By nickel-and-diming you.

In the age of Uber, how can this go on?

Isn't there a better way?

The answer is yes—a better way is here, and it's already an essential part of our everyday lives. It's your smartphone. We're using it not only to search, compare, shop, tweet, snap, post and chat 24/7. We're also using it, and other smart devices, to access nearly everything in our lives — education, healthcare, exercise routines, entertainment, vacation plans, job searches, dates. We don't have to tell you how central the digital realm has become to the way we live now. More and more of us, from Millennials to Baby Boomers, have bought into the Internet of Things—the new world order that is turning our phones, tablets, wearable tech, TVs, cars, refrigerators, and much more into one synchronized computing system. Banks, stuck in an antiquated system of fees and outdated products and services, don't get it that a new technology paradigm has changed how we live our lives. Banks are hellbent on sticking to their passé systems and products because that's how they make money. By sticking it to you.

The Internet of Things has done a lot more than give us streaming video in place of videocassettes or home automation systems in place of mercury-bulb thermostats. It's changed how we experience our world. Sites and apps so different from each other — Facebook, Uber, Amazon, Zappos, YouTube, and Kayak to name a few — give you a world of options. Look at Amazon. It developed Firefly, a technology that lets you scan something with your Fire HDX tablet or Fire phone and buy it through Amazon or its Amazon Price Check app. (Okay, the service would be much more amazing if it let you compare and buy products anywhere online. Someday, somebody's going to come up with that better mousetrap.) Who knows how much shoe leather Zappos and Shoebuy have saved you by letting your "fingers do the walking."

The value of all these apps and sites is greater than the sum of their parts because they also recommend books, movies, shoes, vitamins, household goods, etc., based on your searching habits. Then, when you're ready to buy, you can decide how you're going to pay and when you want delivery. And later on, when you want to purchase another product, you can review an index of your complete buying history. A truly useful app shows you what you're looking for, of course, but it'll also arm you with information.

It's not about the product anymore. It's about you.

We designed a mobile banking app with this customer-centered mantra in mind. When you bank with us at BankMobile, you're getting pretty much the same experience you get from Uber, Amazon, Zappos, and Waze. You'll access your checking account, savings account, line of credit, your financial advisor, and more— the same way you access everything else in your life.

With BankMobile, you'll get an exponentially better way to do your banking. No more nonsense and hype, which is what you get from bank ads all day long.

"We're friendlier."

"We're nicer."

"We care about you."

"We'll give you a cup of coffee."

Gag me.

Instead, our company, BankMobile, is what happens if you take Uber model and apply it to the banking industry. The recipe is simple. Add one measure of communications technology; take advantage of an existing network of ATM machines all over the planet; eliminate the need for branches; *eliminate all of those outrageous fees.*

Use us to help you get to where you want to go — financially.

Stir.

Serve when ready.

That's the BankMobile approach to banking. That's what you're going to hear more about in this book.

#

We've been living and breathing BankMobile since early 2014. That's when we first got to talking about the abuses of our banking system. With tremendous input from our Customers Bank team, we came to a realization. If we couldn't craft a solution to help people learn how to save money, pay off their loans, and live within their means, how were we any better than Bank of America or Chase?

We wrote this book to tell you what makes the big banks tick, why banking with them is a losing game—and where you can find a much better alternative.

First, some introductions are in order. We are Jay Sidhu and Luvleen Sidhu, a father and daughter for twenty-nine years and now a banking team. We have spent a good part of our lives about sixty-five miles west of Philadelphia.

Let's start with Jay.

JAY: I came to this country from India in 1970. My father was an army colonel. He and my mother wanted me to become a doctor so they enrolled me in a pre-med program. Within a week, though, I knew medicine was not for me. I had a different vision: to study business and work in the U.S. I headed to Banares Hindu University for a Bachelors degree in business management. The school was a ten-hour bus ride due east from New Delhi, to Uttar Pradesh.

It was the best decision I ever made. During my junior year, at age 18, I had a life-changing experience when I decided to hitch-hike all the way from Delhi to London and back again in three months, on a budget of less than one hundred dollars. That trip was one of my best learning experiences ever.

After I graduated, I applied to forty American business schools, but I had a big problem: money. I couldn't afford the twenty-dollar fee per application. I wrote to each of the admissions offices and explained my situation. Only one school, Wilkes College (now Wilkes University) in Wilkes-Barre, Pennsylvania, responded—and they went well beyond the call of duty by offering me a scholarship. I was over the moon.

I arrived on Labor Day, a day before classes started. Little did I know that the school, and nearly every other institution in the country, would be closed that day. I didn't know a soul. I wandered past the college library and administrative offices in a state of panic. I came to River Street and to the eastern bank of the Susquehanna River. I sat down next to my suitcase and cried. All I could think was, "What the hell have I done?"

What could I do? I regrouped. I got up and went looking for some kind of solution. I crossed the campus to the corner of South Franklin and West Northampton and came face to face with the Wilkes-Barre Family YMCA. It was an imposing brick building with a "1934" cornerstone. To a twenty-year-old who had never been inside an American building, it was utterly intimidating. But it was open! I went inside and found out that the Y ran a shelter for homeless men. Well, I was a homeless man. That's where I spent my first night in America. But that awful first day was the beginning of a wonderful life for me.

LUVLEEN: I haven't had anything like my dad's immigrant struggles. His courage and his desire to come to the United States paved the way for many personal and educational opportunities for me. The fact is, I have always been given the freedom to "follow my bliss." I attended Harvard thinking I wanted to study medicine, but my class in Organic Chemistry told me I was barking up the wrong tree. I was free to choose another path.

I got selected for the sophomore program at Lehman Brothers and worked there for two summers. I graduated from Harvard with a B.A. in Government.

After college, I became an investment analyst at Neuberger Berman and learned pretty quickly that sitting behind a computer and crunching numbers definitely was not my path. I moved on to a job as a consultant at Booz & Company, in their financial services practice. Sorry! I wasn't any happier there. I realized that just creating pitch books for clients was not my cup of tea. I wanted to build things.

I was starting to feel that, despite all my advantages, I did not have a place in the world. Frustrated with my life and myself, I chose the route I had been avoiding my whole professional life: I went to work in the "family business." There was a job opening for a director of corporate development at Customers Bank. I accepted it—and enjoyed it.

But I wanted to go to graduate school. I studied for an MBA at Wharton and I'm glad I did. It was a great experience.

After earning my MBA, I took four months off to travel around the world. Traveling was absolutely great, and it opened my eyes to educational opportunities I had never considered before. For example, I discovered I had a vision. I wanted people in my generation to become financially literate. And I wanted to work with my dad to help him innovate within the banking industry. We both agreed I should rejoin Customers Bank and focus my efforts on creating the same "wow" experience we all have when we're using our favorite apps.

When I was at business school, I walked into the branch office of a bank to open my first checking account. I was astounded: It took me twenty-five minutes to open the account! I couldn't understand. I had booked a ticket to Australia on Orbitz the day before in less than five minutes.

Before I left the branch, I asked one of the bank associates if she could recommend some products that might make financial sense for me to have. She handed me a generic sheet of paper listing all the bank's products. That's it. No advice. No personalization.

I could not believe banking was so old-school. So out of touch with the kind of technological advances my friends and I took for granted. I walked out of that bank and thought, "This has got to change."

I was really excited to begin working for Customers Bank. I couldn't wait to start working on my ideas. I was going to put together a team that would make banking as affordable and effortless as Orbitz. And I knew I would have Dad's support.

To my great surprise, I really loved my job and our awesome team. We loved working on a project that we knew could change people's lives for the better. What drives me to make BankMobile take off is my belief that people deserve to feel financially empowered. BankMobile can help that happen. It hurts me to say it, but the industry that gave my father so much has become the industry that is thwarting all too many of my creative and enterprising friends. I want to do my small part to help turn things around for them and the rest of our generation.

To that end, I now serve as chief strategy officer at BankMobile. I work with incredible people who are using their business acumen and social commitment to disrupt an industry crying out for innovation. We are all working to develop a business model that provides a stellar banking experience to our customers, is much more affordable, gives access to 55,000-plus ATMs across America for free, pays higher interest on savings, and empowers people through financial literacy—all while allowing the bank to stay profitable. We will innovate and empower our customers by offering a banking service that is easier to use and more convenient than any other bank's offerings—they are simply better than anything else available in America. That's what all the great start-ups of the past ten years have done. That's what we want BankMobile to do too. I believe that with my dad's forty years in the banking industry and my passion to think creatively about the big financial problems, we will shake this business up.

If you want to see for yourself how we are determined to transform the banking industry, keep reading. We've got an exciting story to tell you.

CHAPTER 1

Banks Are Pathetically out of Step with the Age of Uber

WE WANT YOU TO KNOW ABOUT A BEAUTIFUL BUSINESS.

The banking business.

Sure, we just got done saying how your bank is ripping you off. But banks weren't always part of a greedy monopoly. They weren't always indifferent to your hardships and aspirations. Banks used to care about communities and businesses. They knew life was a two-way street: They needed you; you needed them.

As bad as things have gotten in recent years—and they've gotten bad, what with the financial crisis in the U.S. and banking implosions in the U.K., Belgium, Iceland, Russia, Ukraine, Spain, Ireland, Venezuela, and Greece—there's no way around it. You need a bank. Everybody needs a bank.

Whether you are eighteen or eighty-one, a college professor, a short-order cook or a student, you need a safe place to put your money. And you need help managing it. At some point, you may need a mortgage, a business loan, a college loan, an investment strategy, a retirement plan, and you'll certainly need money to raise a family. No institution can give you access to money—and help you live out your personal, professional and financial dreams—the way a bank can.

We know many of you don't love banks. That's because you did not experience the beautiful business that I (Jay) entered as a twenty-two-year-old MBA graduate of the commerce department of Wilkes College (now the Jay S. Sidhu School of Business and Leadership). We young bank associates lived by a simple code: Protect your customers' money and manage risks prudently. Anyone who lived through the 2008 financial crisis will appreciate those eight little words.

Back in the early 2000s, the big banks were doing everything but managing risk. And the industry had become anything but beautiful. The J.P. Morgan Chases, Citis, Bank of Americas, and numerous others got into the high-stakes gambling business—and our economy went kerplunk. In fact, it's believed that a J.P. Morgan economist designed the complicated derivative called the credit default swap that threatened to overturn the economy. Created, perhaps, to help Exxon pay for the Exxon Valdez oil spill, the credit default swap gained traction in the sub-prime mortgage market, where it got bundled into other financial instruments and resold so many times that the original buyer and seller no longer had any relationship with each other. These assets were so complicated that *to this day*

Lehman Brothers—the banking giant that had $619 billion in debt when it filed for bankruptcy at the height of the subprime mortgage crisis— still has a team in place working to unravel them and pay back creditors 26.9 cents on the dollar. We wouldn't be surprised if the odds at Trump Taj Mahal are better than that.

#

JAY: I left the banking industry in 2006—before the credit default swap madness—to spend time with my brother Harry. He had been diagnosed with leukemia. There's nothing like a family health crisis to push your career ambitions onto the back burner. My sister Hareeta reacted much the same way I did. But she went a step further: She became Harry's bone marrow transplant donor. The three of us had always been close, but now that Harry's health was in jeopardy, we went into a huddle. Nothing mattered more than getting Harry back on his feet again.

Amazingly, Harry's health improved. To celebrate, we chose the number-one item on our bucket list: a trip around the world. One of our long stopovers was in our native India. When we returned to the States, I had a strong desire to preserve the high I gained by experiencing new people and places. One way to do that: Keep away from the banking industry! I played a lot of golf. And I got commitments for $500 million for a private equity fund for possible investments in troubled banks.

But by 2009, when I was fifty-eight, I decided I simply was not ready for the early-bird special. I decided to put my money where my mouth was and get back in the saddle.

My first project was Atlantic Coast Financial Corp., a retail bank headquartered in Jacksonville, Florida, that we put through a recapitalization plan. I'm gratified that it is flourishing now.

My second project came in 2013, when I initially raised $17 million from friends for New Century Bank, a distressed bank in Pennsylvania. The board and my fellow investors asked me to become CEO and I accepted with gratitude and enthusiasm. We renamed the bank Customers Bank and created its holding company, Customers Bancorp, Inc. Our name was meant to remind us who we were serving.

An awful lot had happened in my years away from banking. First, the country suffered the financial crisis of 2007-2009. *People* suffered. Stock markets around the world went into a tailspin and many people who had worked hard and saved scrupulously saw their 401(k)s shrink by as much as fifty percent. The housing market, at the mercy of the credit default swap gambit, tanked too, and 7.5 million Americans owed more on their mortgages than their homes were worth. With their houses underwater, nearly one-fifth of homeowners were vulnerable to foreclosure. By the end of 2008, some 2.6 million people had lost their jobs. The unemployment rate rose to 7.2 percent—the highest rate since January 1993 and the highest yearly job-loss total since 1945. Some Baby Boomers moved back in with their elderly parents. Some GenXers, GenYers, and Millennials moved back in with their Baby Boomer parents. One 2008 survey reported that more than 76 percent of homeowners and renters who moved because of foreclosures were staying with family or friends.

When we say "homeowners," "renters," "Baby Boomers," "GenXers," "GenYers," and "Millennials," we're talking about you. About us.

Second, seismic changes in technology sent shock waves through virtually every industry imaginable. When I went into semi-retirement in 2006, Zappos had been around for seven years, iTunes five, Skype three, LinkedIn three, and GrubHub two. Facebook was only two years old and Twitter was ready to roll. Smartphones were a novelty.

Then came a tsunami of technological change: the iPhone in 2007, Spotify in 2008, WhatsApp in 2009, Uber in 2010, the iPad in 2010, and Waze in 2011. There was no hiding from the big question: How can we make a bank as exciting, customer-focused, and easy-to-use as all of these technologies? We saw that the Amazons, Airbnbs, and Ubers of the world had transformed the way we think about products and brands. We no longer buy *things*. We buy *experiences*. Everybody now has higher expectations, not only for products but for how they are delivered, paid for, and consumed.

#

My intentions to turn my corner of the banking world into a high-tech start-up were good. The problem: retail banking had gotten so damn expensive. But if technology was eliminating so many physical stores, why wasn't it doing the same to bank branches?

The only way big banks can hold onto their branch network is by passing their upkeep on to you, the customer. This explains why they charged you $32 billion in overdraft fees in 2013. (The three biggest banks—J.P. Morgan Chase, Bank of America, and Wells Fargo—rang up about $4.4 billion in the first three months of 2015 alone.) And don't think the banks got nicer because their overdraft revenue dropped from an all-time high in 2009 of $37.1 billion. In 2010, Federal regulators crafted legislation to restrain banks from going fee-crazy on you. What the Feds unintentionally did, though, was whack the beehive. The banks began stinging their customers with higher *individual* fees. In short, you paid $26 for an overdraft in 2009 and $35 by May 2015.

The media spotlight on sky-high overdraft fees forced banks to reduce them—by one percent! The big banks weren't going to take that loss in revenue lying down. They came up with a number of other ways to get it back:

- **They increased monthly maintenance fees.** These fees are up by 18 cents, to an average of $12.87. As of 2014, an average checking account cost $154.44 a year to maintain.

- **They raised the minimum balance necessary to qualify for a fee waiver.** The average minimum balance increased by $268.76 in the second half of 2014 to $5,708.76.

- **They upped ATM fees.** The average fee for customers using an out-of-network machine increased by 9 cents, to $1.61. The average surcharge for non-customers using a bank's ATM increased by 14 cents, to $2.65 (as of 2014). Using an out-of-network ATM in Atlanta and New York can cost you between $5 and $8 (as of October 2015).

But wait. There's more. Banks will also charge you for:

- Reordering checks;

- Handling a returned check;

- Owning a debit card;

- Replacing a lost debit card;

- Requesting a print copy of your statement;

- Making a mobile deposit;

- Accessing your money within two business days;

- Getting an email notification of a wire transfer;

- Depositing large amounts of cash;

- Forgetting to update your email address;

- Closing an account within months of opening it;

- Converting dollars into foreign currency to use on an overseas vacation (you can pay up to 20 percent in hidden fees for this);

- Redeeming your reward points (we had trouble believing this one—but it's true.

American Express charges fees for its domestic frequent flier program. Wells Fargo charges you for each airline ticket issued through the bank's rewards vendor).

Why not let the banks speak for themselves? Here's just one paragraph of a small-print disclosure from Capital One 360(R). Keep in mind that it is one of the more "progressive" banks:

"If, at your request, we generate an overnight check as described in the 360 Checking Agreement (see "Overnight a Check"

section), we will charge you $20.00. If, at your request, we place a stop payment on a check that was created on your behalf through Bill Pay, Mail a Check, or Paper Checks we will charge you $25.00. If, at your request, we expedite sending you a 360 Checking Card, we will charge you $25.00. If we agree to transact a wire transfer for you, we will charge you up to $40.00. If you write a check in an amount that exceeds your Available Balance plus any available Overdraft Line of Credit amount at the time the check is presented to us for payment, we'll reject the check and impose an insufficient funds charge in the amount of $9.00."

And here's how J.P. Morgan Chase—the proud inventor of "relationship banking"—talks to you in its small print about overdrafts:

"You must immediately pay the amount of any overdraft along with any fees that apply. If you don't, you may be charged additional fees or interest. We also may report you to credit reporting agencies, close your account, or both. This could affect your ability to open accounts with us or other banks in the future."

Baby, where did our love go?

Banks know you're going to overdraw your account some day. On holidays. Vacations. At the start of a new school year. That's why all but eight of the fifty largest U.S. banks charge fees for ATM or debit point-of-sale overdrafts. Those eight banks restrict high-to-low transaction reordering. But guess what? They don't prohibit it. That means a bank can process your big-ticket mortgage withdrawal first, even if your direct-deposit check shows up in your ledger *before* your mortgage payment is due. The law requires banks to make direct deposits available by the next business day, but it doesn't prevent them from processing all of your pending withdrawals before crediting your deposit.

Transaction reordering has become so much a part of banking DNA that J.P. Morgan Chase was forced to address it in its January 30, 2015, "Important Notices" disclosure. See if this makes any sense to you:

> "*J.P. Morgan Chase will first add deposits to your account and only then subtract wire transfers, non-repeating ("everyday") debit card transactions, online banking transactions, ATM withdrawals, teller cash withdrawals, and* **checks you write that are either cashed or deposited at a teller station by a Chase employee,** *in the order in which they are authorized, withdrawn, cashed or deposited. But* **for any checks you write that are either cashed or deposited at an ATM,** *the bank will subtract withdrawals starting with those having the highest dollar amount and moving to the lowest. The bank reserves the right to use a different order in certain states." (Boldface ours.)*

Huh? Why penalize you for using a machine instead of a person to do your basic banking?

Simple. Transaction reordering is just too lucrative to give up. It increases the possibility that you'll provoke an overdraft. A large transaction like a mortgage payment can reduce your account balance to penalty levels. Making smaller transactions will trigger a cascade of overdrafts and you'll be hit with a fee for each one of them.

#

Do banks really believe they will be the one brick-and-mortar outlier in an ever-rising digital tide?

What's weird is that banks know what role mobile technology plays in our lives. Back in 2012, Bank of America documented the growing popularity of mobile devices for shopping. Bank of America determined that 67 percent of the people they polled used their smartphones to find store locations; 59 percent to compare prices; etc. It also evaluated the growing incidence of near field communication (NFC) technologies to facilitate retail payments via smartphone, as well as bar code software applications to enable comparison shopping. They actually classified mobile tech as a "business necessity."

Bank of America knows how addicted its 15 million active mobile banking customers are to their smartphones. Its 2014 study found that 85 percent of survey respondents checked their smartphone at least a few times a day while 35 percent checked it constantly. Some 79 percent said they'd be willing to give up alcohol or chocolate in order to retrieve their smartphone if it were unexpectedly taken away from them. Asked to rank what was most important to their daily lives, 96 percent of Millennials between 18 and 24 gave their mobile phone top billing. Deodorant clocked in at 90 percent.

At Bank of America, there is a serious disconnect between knowing and doing. In 2014, it published a "Trends in Consumer

Mobility Report" revealing that 47 percent of its survey respondents used either *mobile* or *online* as their primary method of banking. If BoA executives had read their own report, surely they would have to encourage their customers to download a fee-free, easy-to-use, time-saving mobile app to open and close checking accounts, make deposits, withdraw funds, save money, pay off debt, speak with a banking associate, and resolve problems. They would have constructed a business model that would encourage the unbanked and underbanked to participate in a banking system that serves rather than impoverishes them. If they'd have done that, how fast do you suppose that 47 percent figure would have grown to surpass the percentage of Millennials that depend more on their smartphone than deodorant?

Despite its surveys and reports, the banking industry stubbornly refuses to see how the app companies have redefined customer expectations. Amazon understood the need to delight its customers as far back as 1999, when it patented the one-click buying experience. It fought Barnes & Noble tooth and nail to maintain a monopoly over this technique, going so far as to sue B&N for patent infringement. True, other online companies offer one-click buying, but only because they have purchased a software license from Amazon to do so.

Mobile tech is all about speed, convenience, and personalization. It boggles the mind that analog-era recommenders such as the Book-of-the-Month Club and Quality Paperback Book Club are still hanging on in an age when Amazon algorithms are designed to recommend book titles based on your Amazon viewing habits. Whatever makes buying a book—or just about anything else—easy, fast, personal, and fun will find its way into the Amazon business network, which explains why Amazon bought Goodreads, the book discussion and recommender website, in 2013. We won't comment here on Amazon's recent acrimonious relationship with book publishers and authors, except to say that millions of satisfied customers have given Amazon the clout to set prices and distribution practices on their behalf.

Amazon is so aligned with delivering goods and services quickly, easily, and at reasonable prices that between 1999 and 2014, it acquired Alexa Internet, a web traffic data analytics company (1999); Audible, an audio entertainment company (2008); Zappos, an online shoe store (2009); Quidsi, a home and health products delivery company (2010); Woot, a daily deal company (2010); Kiva Systems, a logistics and fulfillment company (2012); and twitch. tv, a live gaming company (2014). What brick-and-mortar bank can boast that it is delivering innovative financial services, growing market share, and retaining customer loyalty the way Amazon and its acquisitions can?

Without exception, every successful customer-friendly, web-based company has taken a page from Amazon's playbook:

- **Uber** is using geolocation-enabled services to provide greater convenience and personalization—and the taxi industry is running scared. Because with Uber you know where your cab is, how long it will take to arrive, and who is driving it, it has made the process of hailing a ride arguably safer and more efficient. And if your driver yells at you because he can't figure out where you're going, Uber will refund your fare.

- The speed, convenience, and personalization that **Netflix** offers its 50 million subscribers have made it successful enough to eat into TV and movie theater profits.

- **Dropbox**, a file-sharing system, lets you share and access your computer files from your laptop, tablet, or mobile phone—eliminating the need to carry around a flash drive (which was an extraordinary product for its time).

- The major airlines that created **Orbitz** in 2001 understood that sites like Travelocity and Expedia were going to eat the travel-booking industry's lunch. We're big fans of Orbitz. You can book flights, make hotel reservations, rent cars, and rate your online experience in one fell swoop.

- The smart **Nest** thermostat syncs with your mobile phone, learns your usage patterns, and helps you conserve energy. Nest is now working on a platform to let refrigerators, TVs, and lightbulbs interact with smart thermostats, smoke alarms, and security cameras, to create a unified home-monitoring system.

In a world of smart devices, these companies are the rule, not the exception. And these companies rule.

"Fast," "convenient" and "personal" have made Google Maps, Facebook, YouTube, Google+, WeChat, Twitter, Skype, Facebook Messenger, WhatsApp, and Instagram the most frequently used smartphone apps. Even smaller enterprises have profited from going miniature: Seamless and GrubHub will deliver food from your favorite local restaurants to your door. Video-game companies offer companion apps for your mobile devices so you can keep track of your playing stats and the progression of in-game characters. The Johnson & Johnson Official 7 Minute app zaps your excuses about not having enough time to exercise because it puts your workout regimen literally at your fingertips.

Companies that want to be significant in the age of mobility have to get behind "easy, fast, personal, and fun." Coca-Cola (born in 1892) hitched its wagon to Amazon's star when it permitted the online retail to start selling 16-ounce cans of Surge, a brand-new citrus flavored soft drink. Pepsi-Cola (born in 1902) developed Pepsi True, a "new kind of cola," set for Amazon distribution in 2015. Both Coke and Pepsi are using Amazon as a virtual test market before stocking their new products on shelves at convenience stores, supermarkets, and big box retailers. Surge is already an Amazon best seller.

Advances in technology, especially in the area of cloud and cognitive, are changing industries and human expectations at warp speed. Pretending that nothing much has changed in twenty or ten or five years is just business suicide. And pay attention! What is considered "easy, fast, personal, and fun" in one decade may be the creaky old man in the next. Blockbuster, the movie and videogame rental company, was once *the* company for video rentals. At its height in 2004, Blockbuster had 60,000 employees and 9,000 store outlets. By 2009, it was struggling to survive against Netflix, which brought those same movies and videogames directly into your mailbox. Even when Netflix fell out of favor by charging one subscription fee for its DVDs and another for its streaming service, it rebounded pretty fast. One, subscribers could still keep DVDs for as long as they liked without incurring any penalty. Two, they fell in love with Netflix all over again when the company began streaming *House of Cards* and *Orange Is the New Black* — original content. Netflix's subscribers may have complained at a certain point, but no matter how disgruntled they were, you know what? They weren't lining up for movies and games at Blockbuster anymore.

The rise and fall of Blockbuster provides a cautionary tale for the banking industry. At first, Blockbuster—a brick-and-mortar store—had a stranglehold on video rentals. In due time competition arrived by way of Netflix, which offered a different and better experience. How did Blockbuster respond? By sticking to its arthritic business model and opening more stores. Ultimately, this landed the company in the morgue.

The big banks may be spared Blockbuster's doom, but as the prevalence of shadow banking outfits such as payday lenders and check cashers have shown, even banks will have to change or they risk becoming irrelevant.

Blockbuster and banks such as J.P. Morgan Chase can also thank the Warby Parker business model for making them anachronisms. As you probably know, Warby Parker is an online purveyor of prescription eyeglasses and sunglasses. To see how a particular pair of glasses looks on your face, you upload a picture of yourself to warbyparker.com and "try them on" by superimposing them over your photo. The company then sends you up to five of your favorite frames. You can then post some selfies to Twitter, Instagram, etc. and crowdsource your friends' opinions. You can even ask Warby Parker associates their opinion by uploading your selfies to the company Facebook page. A la Zappos, you keep the pair you like and send the other four back to the company.

If you want in-store help, you can get it at Warby Parker's retail outlets across the country. Even here, though, where having branch offices actually makes sense, the company has thirteen, not thousands. With the money it has saved by limiting its physical presence, Warby Parker has already donated one million pairs of eyeglasses to men, women, and children in the developing world. The economic impact of WP's philanthropic commitments adds up to $200 million! Later in the book, we'll tell you how Warby Parker has inspired us to be "part profit-oriented and part purpose-oriented." We believe that this make-your-mark blend of business and philanthropy is the model of the future.

It's not enough for banks to party like it's 1999. Banks have to embed themselves in an economic infrastructure that lets everyone flash a smartphone or tablet at a payment reader and buy a cup of coffee, pay a bill, take out a loan, repay a loan, transfer funds from one account to another, and make financial investments. We need to see a banking makeover that will turn your bank into an experience as terrific as the ones Uber, Zappos, Orbitz, Groupon, and Instagram give you. Where the necessary innovations will come from — we cannot say. Innovation is not a jog, it's a marathon. But we know one thing for sure. It won't come from the banking industry, which is as retro as a floppy disk.

#

In the upcoming chapters, we'll tell you how banks make their money and why they refuse to change. We'll talk about the

Millennial generation and the unique financial challenges they face as they try to save money and pay off their college loans. We'll examine how the banks have taken regulatory revenge against the middle class, the underbanked, and the unbanked, striking back at the very people the post-bailout reform was supposed to protect. We'll demystify mobile banking and introduce you to BankMobile, the mobile banking app we designed to *free you of unnecessary bank service fees and minimums.* It's the app that I (Luvleen) left my job at Booz and Company for because I know first-hand how Millennials suffer for lack of actionable financial information and access to capital to start a business. We'll also share with you our vision of a banking ecosystem that will connect your BankMobile checking account with your favorite apps and retailers. And even if, for some reason, you're not persuaded by the amazingness of our app, we have practical advice for you about using your current bank to your own best advantage.

As Jay's mother used to say, a life without money is a bitter life. The banking industry has a once-in-a-hundred-year opportunity to join the Uber era and help make your life sweet. Only time will tell if the banks have the motivation to change. But you—Millennials, GenXers, and tech-savvy Baby Boomers—*you* have the power to motivate them because you are holding the mobile banking revolution in the palm of your hand.

CHAPTER 2

Why Financial Institutions Can't (or Won't) Change— and What That Means to You

JON, 29, STARTED A BACHELORS PROGRAM IN ART AT A pricy college in Boston. Tuition rose and he dropped out to work as a restaurant manager and bartender. His goal was to save money and re-enroll in a less expensive school. In due time, he matriculated at a local, less expensive school in Connecticut. He took out a loan. And he majored in marketing and communications, which he believed to be a more marketable course of study than fine arts.

Now employed full-time by an events marketing company and moonlighting in the events industry, Jon is slowly paying off his college debt. He uses a debit card for daily expenses. He has maxed out his credit cards and concedes that if he lost his job, he could not live comfortably for more than a week. He says he's burdened by his school loans, which will take fifteen years to repay. Even though he participates in direct deposit, his bank processes his debits first, drains his account, hits him with fees for each debit, and only then deposits his paycheck. When Jon travels for work and uses an out-of-network ATM, he has to pay a two-dollar fee on each transaction, on top of the fees the bank that owns the ATM charges. Sometimes that adds up to $3 to $6 just to withdraw his own money! Jon has argued with his bank to void the fees, and sometimes the phone call was worth the effort. If he doesn't watch his checking account like a hawk, he gets hit with overdraft fees.

Why does Jon's bank have to snag him at every turn?

Earlier, we said that banks weren't always heartless and greedy, and it's true. So, how did they get that way? And why don't they change?

To explain the current state of banking, we have to go back to the financial crisis of 2008. In the years leading up to it, big banks had been making housing loans to people who couldn't afford to repay them. If the purpose of a commercial bank is to allocate funds from savers to borrowers in a safe, efficient manner, why were banks so reckless?

You don't have to be Warren Buffet to understand why. Financial institutions approved subprime mortgages to attract more customers. Banks figured they would in turn sell the subprime mortgage debt to other financial institutions, even at risk of spreading bad loans all throughout the banking and investment network. Short term, the tactic worked. Banks and brokers collected billions.

To underscore how badly designed—and how toxic—these loans were, we need only mention the names of once towering companies and government agencies that crumpled under the weight of this mortgage debt: Bear Stearns, Lehman Brothers, Fannie Mae, and Freddie Mac.

The bankruptcies that sank these firms and agencies were just the tip of the iceberg. All told, fifty-eight banks, insurance companies, mortgage lenders, and savings and loans were bought out by other wealthier financial organizations, taken over by the government, or liquidated outright. Here's a sampling of companies that went under as a result of the financial crisis:

- **Countrywide Financial** (Calabasas, CA). Mortgage lender. Bought by Bank of America (Charlotte, NC).
- **Bear Sterns** (NYC). Investment bank. Bought by J.P. Morgan Chase (NYC).
- **Washington Mutual**. Savings and loan association. Bought by J.P. Morgan Chase (NYC).
- **Merrill Lynch** (NYC). Investment bank. Bought by Bank of America (Charlotte, NC).
- **American International Group** (NY). Insurance company. Bailed out by the U.S. federal government.
- **Fannie Mae** (Federal National Mortgage Association) and **Freddie Mac** (Federal Home Loan Mortgage Corporation). Taken over by the Federal Housing Finance Agency.
- **Wachovia** (Charlotte, NC). Retail and investment bank. Bought by Wells Fargo (San Francisco, CA).
- **Lehman Brothers** (NYC). Went bankrupt.
- **Hundreds of community banks around the country.**

All hell was breaking loose. The Feds had to do something. In October 2008, the U.S. Congress passed the Emergency Economic Stabilization Act to create the Troubled Asset Relief Program (TARP), a fund that gave the U.S. Treasury $700 billion to invest in banks or to buy mortgage-backed securities from financial institutions crippled by debt.

Lest the economy suffer complete paralysis, the federal government bailed out banks deemed "too big to fail." We don't really have a problem with that. The FDIC guarantees the safety of accounts up to $250,000, so it had a fiduciary responsibility to make good on its promise to depositors. But TARP came too late for the 2.9 million homeowners who lost their homes in 2009 alone—and for the 21 million Americans who lost their jobs between September 2008 and July 2012. Forty million people suddenly found themselves living below the poverty line.

Congress went on to pass the Dodd-Frank Wall Street Reform and Consumer Protection Act (2010), legislation crafted to keep an eye on institutions too big to fail. The act established lots of new government agencies, including the Financial Stability Oversight Council, the Orderly Liquidation Authority, and the Federal Insurance Office. The new Consumer Financial Protection Bureau was supposed to prevent predatory mortgage lending and insure that disclosures from mortgages, credit card companies, and other financial services providers would be written in layman's language.

So, how's Dodd-Frank been working out for ya?

The big banks are bigger than ever. They still gamble with FDIC-insured money. And they still lend credit default swaps.

Nothing has changed. As was the case with the 2008 mortgage crisis, companies still don't know who owns these swaps or who stands to benefit from a default.

Let's not kid ourselves. The motives of swap investors can be downright sinister. Take the case of Forest Oil Corp, an oil company struggling to stay afloat. In 2014, it was in merger talks with Sabine Oil & Gas, a more solvent competitor, when it learned from some of its shareholders that swap investors were betting on a default *and* buying up stock in order to vote against a merger that could save Forest Oil. Why save a company when killing it will bring you billions? (Forest Oil did end up merging with Sabine Oil & Gas in May 2014.)

And you wonder why the economy still hasn't fully recovered from the 2008 financial debacle!

We see another problem with Dodd-Frank. The 2010 regulations written to watchdog the big banks have actually trickled down to the community banks that did *not* cause the financial crisis. In fact, the 2008 forced mergers of failing banks, along with the growth of nationwide banking, are edging out the community bank.

Originally, community banks were granted charters so that local customers could get loans to buy houses or start small businesses. Now that big regional banks can operate anywhere in the country, they're dominating a lot of markets. Meanwhile, medium and small banks have a hard time complying with all of Dodd-Frank's reporting and compliance rules. The Act threatens to destroy the smaller banks that help grow small businesses and help local communities flourish.

Back to Jon, a Millennial beginning his professional life in the wake of the biggest economic meltdown since the Great Depression. When he entered college the first time around, Jon knew very little about a banking system that gambled with trillions of dollars, got a bailout to pay off its debts, and then continued merrily along with a brick-and-mortar business model that almost every other industry has been replaced with high-tech business models. It became increasingly clear to Jon that banks weren't interested in exploring technological innovations that would result in providing him with a safe place to deposit his money and teach him how to pay off his debt. What would their incentive be? Big banks can take risks on behalf of their wealthiest clients without worrying about any long-lasting consequences—at least not for them. The consequences for people like Jon, however, can be undermining and long-lasting.

We never thought we'd see the day when Charles Koch, the multibillionaire businessman who oversees an industrial empire stocked with oil refining operations, fertilizers, commodity trading services, and a bunch of famous brands (Stainmaster, Quilted Northern, Dixie Cup), would accuse the big banks of taking "corporate welfare." That's what Koch calls the federal bailout. At an August 2015 gathering of wealthy conservatives, Koch said, "We're headed toward a two-tiered society—a society that's destroying opportunities for the disadvantaged and creating welfare for the rich. Misguided policies are creating a permanent underclass, crippling our economy and corrupting the business community."

When Charles Koch points an accusing finger at the big banks, you know that the American Dream, whether home ownership or higher education, is in jeopardy for millions of people.

#

Max, 26, a former product designer and director of marketing for a Brooklyn, N.Y.-based manufacturer, experienced "terrible customer service" when he called his credit card company about a fraudulent charge on his statement. He was stunned to learn that the customer service rep did not know about Regulation Z, a Truth in Lending provision that requires lenders and creditors to disclose all of the specifics of home, auto, and credit card loans. The customer rep sided with the fraudster! Max had initially chosen his credit card as a college student, because of the mileage points that came with sign-up. Now an older and wiser MBA candidate, he intends to investigate customer service before signing up for a new credit card.

Unfortunately, Max's credit card experience isn't unique. A banking system that refuses to innovate retains its ignorant bank employees. Even bank executives don't know much about banking. They're often employees who got moved up through the ranks. Promoting from within would be fine if the banks insisted on continuing-education training programs. How do banks expect their employees to understand the national and global economic environment? How do they expect them to know the fundamentals of good banking practice? Our everyday work experience can't teach us what we need to know, especially when a typical 24-hour news cycle includes stories about China's devaluation of the yuan, Google's strategic reorganization, soaring prices in the commercial real estate market, an expected rise in short-term interest rates by the Federal Reserve, and controversy over an international bailout of the Greek economy. Banks need to educate and train their employees—but they don't. So what do bank employees end up doing? They learn from their ill-informed peers. If they see their colleagues taking dangerous risks, they do the same.

#

You'd have to be living on Alpha Centauri to think the technologies of the past eight years haven't radically changed the way we earthlings navigate our world. Banks may be out of step, but they aren't blind. After all, bank executives use smartphones and tablets. They watch movies on Netflix and Amazon Prime. They download books to Kindles and iBooks. They shop with store coupons that arrive digitally and pay with Apple Pay and Android Pay. They use Waze when they drive and Orbitz when they fly. They themselves personally experience the ease and pleasure of tapping an app to make something wonderful happen.

So why don't they adapt smart device technologies to the banking business?

Because they can't sacrifice the sacred cow that's been so good to them for so long.

IBM had the hardest time sacrificing its own sacred cow, the mainframe. That's how IBM lost millions, possibly billions, on PCs and routers—the innovative technologies of their day. In more recent years, IBM has been careful not to fudge it again. In the early 2000s, it refashioned itself as a business consulting services company geared to a "flat" integrated economic landscape of manufacturers, inventors, labor, and consumers. It sold off its unprofitable PC unit in 2004 and its low-end server division in

2014—and now IBM makes seven billion dollars a year from cloud computing services alone.

You might not have been born yet when Microsoft was obsessed with its proprietary operating system. When open-source software challenged Microsoft's hegemony, the company broadened its focus into four strategic areas: operating systems, apps, the cloud, and devices.

Dell, once the big name in desktop computers built to the user's specifications, has remade itself as a provider of IT and networking solutions for the enterprise. Like IBM, it had to let go of the desktop computer when China and other countries turned it into a commodity with low profit margins.

Kodak is a textbook example of a company that struggled to regain its footing in the IT age, even though it claimed to have invented the digital camera. Its core strength was chemicals, but, rightly or wrongly, it retooled itself as an imaging company. For awhile, a high-margin inkjet division replaced film, but in 2013, when that was proving unsustainable, Kodak announced a reorganization plan. Once synonymous with instant photography for the masses, Kodak is barely an afterthought in the consumer market it created and dominated for more than a century.

These four iconic companies have been reengineering their old-industry business models for years. Have the J.P. Morgan Chases and Bank of Americas of the world been doing that, too? We don't believe so. They are making incremental changes: closing some branches, installing video screens or fancier ATMs in others. But all the while they continue to increase the fees you are paying.

Reinventing a company—let alone an industry—is hard. As they powered ahead to regain profitability and relevance, IBM, Microsoft, Dell, and Kodak suffered terrible labor pains. They laid off tens of thousands of employees. They closed cherished divisions. The reinvention of banking will be no less painful. But, without making substantive changes to its business model, banks will be like the last flight out of Da Nang at the end of the Vietnam War: desperate to leave a failed endeavor behind.

Holding onto too many branch offices is only part of the problem. Community—the idea that the branch office used to embody—has changed, too.

Community bankers used to be enmeshed in the lives of their customers. They joined the Rotary Club and the Chamber of Commerce. They developed friendships with local business owners. They knew who got married, who had a baby, who got promoted, who was in the market for a first home. Personally knowing each and every customer was the very definition of community banking.

In the smartphone era, community doesn't limit us to the people we meet in person. Today communities are also virtual groups of people anywhere in the world with similar needs and common interests. Groupon is a great example of a community-oriented business. The company name says it all. It targets a group, or community, of consumers looking for deal-of-the-day coupons.

The most successful online companies and apps provide a platform where you can establish or join a community based on shared interests and values. These range from edible insects to taxidermy—not to mention communities of people you work with or went to college with. A community is simple or complex, private or public, inclusive or exclusive. Your bank's job is to recognize that communities are groups of like-minded people or individuals banded together—teachers, police officers, firefighters, women, students, dog lovers—and help them achieve their financial goals. By creating communities, people are actually aggregating marketplaces for anybody with a relevant product to sell. No need to run focus groups. Your target audience has already defined itself.

America boasts 17.7 million members of labor unions, 100 million members of professional and vocational associations, and 50 million employees of businesses with more than 1,000 employees. Why aren't the banks developing affinity relationships with these communities, and supporting them with charitable donations and relevant products and services? (We'll talk later about how BankMobile is doing just that.)

One bank that gets it is USAA, the San Antonio, Texas-based financial services company that offers banking, investing, and insurance services to people and families that have served in the U.S. military. As of June 30, 2014, USAA Investments had $64.6 billion in USAA mutual fund assets under management. It also managed $60.8 billion in assets.

How many branch offices does USAA have?

Zero. It's a digital bank.

The bank has one full-service banking location in San Antonio. If members in other cities want help opening an online account or need information about USAA's financial services, they can stop in at a regional service location near their military base.

At USAA the sacred cows have long been put out to pasture. USAA was able to do that not only because it knew what digital technology could do for its clients. USAA is also guided by the values of the institution it serves. It takes a disciplined approach to managing money. It focuses on risk management. And it believes that success is measured in years, not months.

Wouldn't it be something if civilian banks took a page from USAA's playbook?

#

Every successful company today is a tech company. You can be selling shoes or news stories or taxi rides, but if you aren't constantly thinking about using every available digital channel to sell, you're going to be sideswiped by somebody else who has made technology the keystone of their business model.

Compare banking to Domino's Pizza, the pizza delivery franchise. Domino's calls itself a tech company. In fact, its biggest department isn't mozzarella cheese—it's IT. You can order pizza from Domino's website. You can order via a voice-activated "personal assistant" named Dom. You can track your pizza from online order to delivery. And now that Domino's has formed a partnership with Ford Motor Company, you can order pizza from the control panel of the Ford Sync. Like all innovative consumer product companies, Domino's understands that food is more popular—and profitable—when people connect it with having fun.

Dealing with your bank: Not fun.

Domino's Pizza, founded in 1960 by two brothers is now managed by Bain Capital, an investment firm that knows older companies tend to get stodgy. That's why Domino's invites creative people—product engineers, app developers, and marketing geniuses—to work with them. There's no rule that says your company has to be its own brain trust.

What Domino's knows is this: Technology is the most effective way for a franchise to communicate with its customers. Smartly applied, tech is the biggest differentiator between companies that run in place and companies that lift off.

#

With so many convincing reasons to embrace fee-free mobile technology, why haven't banks taken the lead of a Domino's Pizza or an Uber or an Amazon?

We think one reason is that banks have become elitist. Banks that once knew every customer by name now don't know you from Adam. They've got bigger fish to fry.

Banks believe they mainly make money by serving high-net-worth individuals and large businesses. They hold onto a large pool of money that sits in checking accounts—and they pay little or no interest on it. They make money from interest charged on larger-than-average mortgages and business loans. And they collect a percentage of the assets other than deposits under their management.

Banks would have to be crazy to nickel-and-dime their wealthy clients with nuisance fees. In fact, top customers can negotiate bank fees concerning closing costs for mortgages, home equity lines, retail loans, or commercial loans.

How are banks treating their Millennial and middle-class customers?

By mismanaging their money. How else to explain the more than $30 billion in overdraft fees that banks made in 2014—fees that banks could eliminate if they stopped punishing their customers for using their own money! Some analysts have estimated that banks are essentially collecting 1,700 percent interest by charging those high fees on overdrawn accounts. It's insane. We wonder why regulators are not focusing on this issue.

The country's three biggest banks are the worst offenders. In the first quarter of 2015, J.P. Morgan Chase, Bank of America, and Wells Fargo made more than $1.1 billion on overdraft fees. By the end of the year, they had charged approximately $4.5 billion. That's about twenty dollars for each American adult.

Unfortunately, overdraft fees are becoming the lifeblood of many smaller banks as well. Woodforest National Bank and First National Bank Texas derive more than 40 percent of their of non-interest revenue from overdraft charges. You won't be surprised to hear that Woodforest operates more than 750 branches in seventeen states; First National operates 280 in three.

A bank analyst at SNL Financial, a Virginia-based financial analysis firm, nailed it when he said, "These banks are highly reliant on these charges. It just points out that's their business model."

Some of this fee-mongering is understandable. Post-2008, banks discovered that loans weren't profitable in a slow-growing economy. To satisfy their shareholders, banks turned to asset management, trading, investment banking, international operations, and mortgage banking. They didn't completely chuck their "relationship" with the middle class, though, because, frankly, when there's money to be made, banks aren't going to leave any of it on the table. Repay your loan a day late, your bank pockets a fee. Repay your loan two days late, your bank pockets two fees. If your bank processes your loan before your cash inputs, you get penalized because your checking account dropped below an arbitrary required minimum balance.

In short, the way banks are using mobile technology today is simply adding to the cost of banking. They are using it to make their customers pay more fees! Millions of Americans cannot pay off their debt, make a down payment on a house, or continue their education. Banking executives have to study how other industries have responded to the digital era by maintaining profitability *and* caring about their customers. If they can help all of their customers succeed—the unbanked, the underbanked, the middle class, the Millennial Generation, small business owners, and the wealthy—they will never have to fail again.

CHAPTER 3

What Millennials Want from Their Bank

SIMON IS A BROOKLYN-BASED GRAPHIC DESIGNER, PART-time college student, and the former guitarist of The Beeters, a punk-rock band. At 33, the only debt he carries is his college loans. Ask Simon about the life he lived in his twenties, though, and you'll get a story about a repo'd car, maxed-out credit cards, and ChexSystems—the background check company that advised banks not to let Simon open a checking or savings account with them because he was a serious credit risk. Now that he has dug himself out of a deep debt hole, Simon loves to talk about the guy he used to be: a twentysomething with extravagant spending habits and little financial know-how.

Simon's descent into debt began as a college student in Los Angeles. In the beginning of freshman year, Capital One offered him his first credit card and he managed his spending we—until he began dating a girl he liked. He began paying for movies, restaurants, and trips with the card and accumulated thousands of dollars of debt even before the two moved in together.

"I made some bad decisions," Simon says about dropping out of college to move in with his girlfriend. After racking up even more debt, they moved to Houston, where they believed they could live more cheaply.

"Little did I know that the labor market in Houston was a lot weaker than in L.A.," Simon says.

They both had trouble finding jobs. Simon ended up selling shoes at a mall. Whatever the two of them made did not begin to cover the cost of the new furniture, the car, and the scores of furnishings they thought they couldn't live without. It all went on a credit card.

"One thing leads to another," he says. "Before you know it, you don't have enough money to pay your bills."

The collections notices arrived every week.

By that point, ChexSystems had blacklisted Simon. Bank of America, his employer's check issuer, let him cash his paychecks but they would not approve his request to open checking and savings accounts.

One day, a teller asked Simon why he didn't have an account with the bank. Simon explained the situation.

"I still don't know why that particular teller made it possible for me to open an account," Simon says. "It probably helped that

I was steadily employed and had created a pattern of cashing my check every two weeks at the same bank."

Bank of America in fact did approve Simon's new checking account with one proviso: He had to attend an eight-hour Chex-Systems class on financial responsibility. He learned tactical tasks, such as balancing a checking account. More important, though, he learned about living within his means.

As for the "zillions" of bank fees he amassed, Simon paid them all off. He assumed complete responsibility for his spendthrift lifestyle and even when he had cause, never asked his bank to void the charges.

At 24, Simon decided to move back home and work in his father's graphic design shop. He considered declaring bankruptcy, but, upon the advice of his parents, he chose instead to pay off his consumer debt little by little. "By now, though, I wasn't starting from zero. I had to climb out of a pit."

Simon doesn't blame anybody but himself. "I wasn't a criminal," he says. "I was just really immature. In the end I had people in my life who helped me get to a place where I could figure things out."

#

Simon is hardly alone in having mismanaged his money, education, and personal life throughout a good part of his twenties. We believe that many of Simon's money mishaps could have been nipped in the bud by a bank that saw itself as his financial advisor. After all, banks collect all kinds of data about their accounts.

Instead of using it to build a case against their uncreditworthy customers, they could analyze patterns of reckless spending and intervene—as counselors, not jailers—to stop it.

And because Millennials have had their digital habits tracked throughout their lives, banks should be using this data to help enrich a generation thrown off its game by a devastating financial crisis. Credit card companies already use algorithms to detect "suspicious" charges to your credit card. Why would you buy a new smart TV in New Jersey when you in fact, live in Michigan? That kind of technology should be applied to your own purchasing habits, too.

Simon's spending scenario is familiar to many other Millennials. Even those who haven't succumbed to wild spending habits know what it's like to carry college debt from one year to the next. Where is the innovation from traditional banks when it comes to student lending? We have seen some important innovation in startups—SoFi, Earnest, and CommonBond, to name a few—but from the banks...nada. Danny Crichton, a doctoral student in public policy at Harvard's John F. Kennedy School of Government, writes, "Imagine if the first thing a traditional bank said to a college graduate and potential new customer was 'open an account, and we can help you refinance your student loans with a lower rate and save serious dollars during repayment.'"

Don't hold your breath.

You gave the banks a helping hand during the 2008 financial crisis. They should do the same for a new generation of bank customers.

#

LUVLEEN: When I was fourteen, Dad used to say he could pinpoint my location by the sound of my flip phone. Every time I checked it, every ten minutes or so, he heard a click-clack as I flipped it open. Seven years later, I got my first smartphone. I will be the first to say that the smartphone influences way more of my life than the flip phone ever did. My iPhone is so much an ever-present reality in my life that if it goes missing even for a moment my heart races.

The flip phone made calling people convenient and it was a good distraction on the bus to school. But, forgetting my flip phone at home didn't feel like I left home naked. Leaving my smartphone behind does. I use it a hundred times more than I ever used my flip phone. And study upon study confirms that I am not an anomaly:

- 80 percent of Millennials say the first thing they do in the morning is reach for their smartphone.
- 87 percent say their smartphone never leaves their side.
- 37 percent use their smartphone camera at least once a day.

The Millennial cohort, born approximately between 1980 and 2000, belongs to a generation of some 75.3 million people who can hardly remember life without computers, gaming devices, and the Internet. The Millennials are distinctive for other reasons, too. They represent the greatest number of college graduates ever, receiving twice as many B.A. degrees in 2009 than graduates in 1970. A less fortunate fact is that a staggering 58 percent of these college graduates report having student debt. Not surprisingly, 36 percent of Millennials — 21.6 million — live in their parents' home, up from 18.5 million of their same- aged counterparts in 2007.

51

JAY: My fellow Baby Boomers will recall that for us, college graduation signaled the start of our financial independence. We got jobs. We rented an apartment with some friends. We began paying off our college loans. That was then. Recently, while having dinner with friends, I learned that all of their twentysomething children were living at home. Between school debt and underemployment, these Millennial college grads could not afford to move out.

Transitioning into adulthood has gotten very expensive.

You might think the Millennials would be the most depressed generation since the days of Herbert Hoover. Yet, even though they have lived through the dot-com bust of 2000 and the financial crisis of 2008, research indicates that Millennials are optimistic about their financial future. Seventy percent aspire to start independent businesses with the help of digital technologies. They admire the rock-star industry disrupters of the past thirty years, including Steve Jobs (Apple), Mark Zuckerberg (Facebook), Jeff Bezos (Amazon), Travis Kalanick (Uber), Daniel Ek (Spotify), Jan Koum (WhatsApp), and others; and they're confident that they can accomplish similar goals, albeit on a smaller scale. They have been shaped by a tough job market and they trust their own individual efforts more than the ups and downs of an unreliable job market.

When Luvleen was approaching college age, her mom and I searched online for college majors most likely to lead to a good career. In 2005, the top major was engineering. A 2015 ranking by the Georgetown University Center on Education and the Workforce shows that the demand for engineers in petroleum, pharmacy, metallurgy, mining, chemistry, electrical, aerospace, mechanical, computing, and geological — hasn't slowed a bit. While these majors were more likely to lead to employment than, say, a major in art history, social work, photography, culinary arts, or music, even they weren't inoculated against a soft job market. The unemployment rate for 18-29 year olds was 13.4 percent in July 2015 (a figure that includes people who have given up looking for work). That stands to reason. Millennials have been shut out of many entry-level jobs. And when they do get hired, they tend to be first-fired in times of corporate belt-tightening. Georgetown, which analyzes U.S. Census data, suggests that "unemployment is becoming a youth problem."

This bad news has convinced many Millennials to abandon the conventional post-college search for a good entry-level job and instead fend for themselves. That's admirable, but they're up against some harsh realities that the Baby Boom and Gen X generations did not have to face.

First, average college-loan debt is in the neighborhood of $30,000. For some recent college grads, that figure soars as high as $116,000.

Second, banks are still stingy when it comes to making loans, especially to young people who haven't repaid their student loans. Millennials are trapped in a Catch-22: Banks don't want to underwrite a small business loan because would-be entrepreneurs have student debt. But aspiring entrepreneurs can't move forward without a loan to finance their projects.

We know entrepreneurial Millennials who work regular day jobs and try to start a business in their off hours. Bank lenders are rejecting their loan requests on the basis of their high debt-to-income ratio. All too many talented Millennials are having a rough time getting their businesses off the ground.

Even Millennials with relatively high levels of income and asset ownership struggle to make debt payments. About 47 percent with outstanding student debt loans are concerned about their ability to pay them off. This is especially true for women (51 percent), part-time workers (57 percent), non-Asian minorities (57 percent), and people with lower income (62 percent). If a well-educated group is struggling, how much more stressful are the lives of Millennials with less education and bills to pay?

I'm not an alarmist. I've seen boom and bust cycles come and go. But given the double whammy of punitive bank fees and personal debt, the situation in late 2015 is more serious than anything I've seen in my lifetime.

The good news is that some smart policy researchers are thinking about ways to alleviate the Millennials' one-trillion-dollar debt burden. One think tank recommends letting young borrowers refinance their student loans. "Lowering interest rates would allow struggling borrowers and would-be entrepreneurs to lower their monthly payments, freeing up income to invest in new businesses," says the D.C.-based Center for American Progress. Without an incentive like this one, many entrepreneurial dreams will never see the light of day.

The fact is, entrepreneurial start-ups from 1996-2012 created by people between twenty and thirty-four were low relative to startups in other generations. Why? Because access to capital and lack of know-how are key barriers to entry. This is terrible news for the 54 percent of young adults who say they want to start a business or have already started one, as well as the 38 percent who have delayed starting a business because of economic factors.

Three years ago, a Finnish economist named Markus Jantti found that children in the United States have less "intergenerational earnings mobility" than children in Denmark, Finland, Norway, Sweden, and, amazingly, the United Kingdom—historically, a country with a rigid class structure. That means that if you live in the U.S. and your parents are poor, you will probably grow up to be poor, too. And so will your children.

Shame on us!

When I arrived in this country as a college student in 1972, I had no idea what my career would be. But I believed in the American promise that if you work hard, you can get ahead. How can Millennials get ahead if the same economic crises that keep poor people poor are holding them back, too? A digital-based economy can and will change this, but banks have to lead the way.

#

Carol, 32, bought her first house in Tacoma, Washington, in 2011. She cobbled together a down payment with a $10,000 gift from her aunt and money she saved over five years as a nurse in a hospital step-down unit. With her long history as a saver, Carol was surprised when she couldn't access the money earmarked for her mortgage from her savings account. When she'd opened the account, she'd assumed her money would be liquid.

"It should have been, but it wasn't," Carol says. "Here I was, ready to take out a mortgage, and my bank is asking me to send them letters and other documentation just so I can take my money out."

The bank, famous for helping customers "keep their own money," advised Carol to open a checking account in her name. At that point, they would "rush" her money to her.

"But there was a catch," Carol says. "I had to pay a significant fee to get my money out 'in a rush.'"

When Carol asked why she had to wait a month to get her money, the tele-rep assigned to her "case" said that the thirty-day transfer period was bank policy.

Carol had to pay a bank fee to get to her own money.

When the funds finally came through, Carol closed out her savings and new checking accounts. Then the bank charged her a fee for closing her checking account within a year of opening it.

Carol is philosophical about her "negative experience" with her former bank. "Nowadays, I'm skeptical when a financial advisor at any bank wants to counsel me about my finances," she says. "From what I've seen, you don't need a whole lot of credentials to give advice. My grandfather, an immigrant from Poland, knows more about finances than financial advisors do!"

#

Carol has managed to save money, continue her education, graduate without debt, and work at a stable healthcare job. A bank should fall all over itself to help somebody like her get a mortgage, especially as Millennials lag behind GenXers and Baby Boomers in home ownership. Over the last decade, Carol's fellow Millennials have decreased their number of home purchases by 7.3 percent, a statistic that also helps explain the relative sluggishness of the U.S. economy. It's a crime that Millennials have been priced out of the housing market in thirteen great American cities: New York, San Francisco, San Jose, San Diego, Los Angeles, Denver, Portland, Boston, Washington, D.C., Seattle, Miami-Fort Lauderdale, Sacramento and Riverside, CA. A typical Millennial in San Diego, for example, has to earn $36,000 a year to afford an average home mortgage. Instead of building equity, Millennials in unaffordable markets are stuck with skyrocketing rents.

"Generation Rent" has a valid reason to avoid home ownership. As children, Millennials saw their parents end up under water, with homes worth less than their mortgage. Who can blame them for being gun bankedshy?

Millennials have taken other hits, too, including stagnating wages, the growth of the freelance "gig" economy, the elimination of full-time work, and the rise of part-time employment. In short, they've gotten trapped in a web (no pun intended) created by the very Internet technologies that now dominate their lives.

As time passes, renting versus owning is going to have a ripple effect throughout society. "If you have a generation that is less committed to taking a risk and buying property [in a particular community], either because there are no jobs or because the overall national situation looks rocky, then [municipalities] . . . absolutely have a problem for . . . long-term obligations to such things as pension funds," says Paul Conwayof Generation Opportunity, a think tank specializing in the economics of the Millennial generation.[1]

We'll see plenty more collateral damage, too. The home-improvement industry will suffer and so will public schools, whose funding depends on property taxes.

If you're thinking that Millennials just can't get their act together, you should know that, according to a MacArthur Foundation survey, 67 percent of surveyed Millennials have either stopped contributing to their retirement savings, gotten a second job, begun working longer hours, or accumulated credit card debt in an effort to "keep a roof over their head."

Interestingly, Zach, a 26-year-old manager of three apartment buildings in Brooklyn and the Bronx, has been saving his salaried earnings for the past two-and-a-half years so he can buy a rental property. Having observed the rental habits of his long-time friends and work colleagues, he expects that owning a multi-family house will give him the cushion he needs to live a financially secure life.

JAY AND LUVLEEN: If you see yourself in this social and economic profile of Millennials, maybe you'll see yourself in their banking profile, too.

Pollsters are already starting to distinguish between Generation Y.1 and Generation Y.2. The former consists of 18-to-24-year-olds,

---

[1] NPR: http://www.npr.org/2012/06/07/154504195/generation-rent-slamming-door-of-homeownership

a group more likely than the overall population to use ATMs. Fiserv, a financial services technology firm, found that these younger Millennials on average visit an ATM 4.3 times a month, compared with 3.4 times a month for all consumers. Fiserv researchers speculate that Gen Y.1-ers have felt the negative impact of credit on their parents and feel more financially in control when they use cash. These young Millennials tend to be unmarried, do not have children, and do not own a house. Their primary concern is, "Do I have enough money to pay my everyday expenses?"

Generation Y.2—twenty-five-to-thirty-four-year-olds—are further along in their personal relationships and careers. One 2014 study found that 64 percent of these older Millennials prefer banking by mobile phone, compared with 56 percent of the younger group. The first generation to fully embrace digital in every corner of their lives—from videogames to phone apps—older Millennials are keen on using alternative services for their checking account needs. In fact, they shun basic checking accounts that nearly always come with monthly fees and penalties. So strong is their distaste for fees that 22 percent of Gen Y.2 Millennials would prefer to use that same money to pay for enhanced security or ID protection instead, compared with 17 percent of the overall population. And—is this crazy?—an overwhelming majority of Millennials (71 percent) would rather go to a dentist than listen to bank "propaganda."

What most Millennials have in common is their rejection of written checks. A 2014 Gallup poll found that 72 percent of Millennials use online banking services every week. Some 64 percent receive at least half of their bills electronically. At the same time, banked and underbanked Millennials maintain an average checking account balance of more than $2,240—possibly to pay off debts such as college loans.

What about the financial health of college-educated Millennials, the subgroup theoretically best equipped to weather economic stress? Shouldn't they be more knowledgeable about personal finance than their non-college-educated peers? Despite having come of age during two financial crises, less than one half of this group has sufficient funds set aside to cover three months of expenses in the event of an unexpected shock. Asked if they could come up with $2,000 to cover an emergency, 30 percent "probably" or "certainly" could not. Most surprising of all is the level of confidence among Millennials regarding their financial literacy. While as many as 85 percent of college-educated Millennials believe they are good at dealing with day-to-day financial matters such as checking accounts, credit and debit cards, and tracking expenses, only 14 percent polled correctly answered five financial literacy questions designed by a U.S. Health and Retirement Study (2008, 2011) about numeracy, inflation, risk diversification, mortgages, and bond prices.

#

The best time to encourage financial literacy, we believe, is before people have developed the kind of habits that get them in trouble with credit cards or other financial issues. So BankMobile is working to spread awareness of financial literacy by offering a Financial Literary Scholarship. Our first recipient was Troy Howard, a student at the University of Wisconsin with a deep interest in the issue of financial literacy.

Troy partnered with a local credit union to offer a "Terror Buck Savings Initiative" at Appleton West High School, a program that encourages students to save money. His other initiatives include Money Smart Week and financial education programs for younger audiences. We're proud of Troy and we want to encourage him and other young people to carry the message of financial literacy to a growing nationwide audience, which is why we provide free financial coaching to college students around the country, preparing them to make prudent financial decisions.

#

As we mentioned earlier, low-socioeconomic-status communities tend not to use traditional banking products such as checking accounts, and they frequently turn to check-cashing facilities and payday loan outfits. But even college-educated Millennials making up to $75,000 a year tend to feel cash-strapped enough to use a prepaid debit card. In this regard, the more privileged members of the generation and the genuinely cash-strapped follow the same pattern of turning toward fee-heavy alternative financial services—a trend much less common among the Gen X, Baby Boomer, and elderly populations.

So, when financial pundits wonder if Millennials will change banking forever, or if Millennials are set to disrupt the banking industry, they are asking themselves some hard questions about the future of banking:

- How is a debt-burdened Millennial generation responding to an abundance of fees and penalties doled out by the big banks?

- What impact is the Millennials' preference for mobile devices having on branch and online banking?

- How do we address the Millennials' greater need for affordable financial literacy and advice, given the economic challenges they face, including the high tuitions they have paid for their education?

- When will banks address the sense of disgust Millennials feel for the banks' lack of transparency and authenticity?

- Why are Millennials across the income spectrum increasingly drawn to non-traditional banking products instead of checking and savings accounts?

We've got some questions too: What's in store for banks when an entire young generation sees no difference between their bank and any other bank? What does it mean when 33 percent of Millennials say that in five years, they won't need a bank at all? What does it say about a generation that would be more excited to use a banking or payments offering from Google, Amazon, Apple, PayPal, or Square than from their own nationwide bank?

It says, "Ladies and Gentlemen of the banking industry, fasten your seat belts. It's going to be a bumpy ride."

CHAPTER 4

What Middle-Class Americans Want from Their Bank

EVE, 53, LOST HER JOB AT A GLOBAL IT ENTERPRISE IN January 2009. She had just begun her twenty-fourth year with the company when she and 200 fellow employees were cut in what the Bureau of Labor Statistics refers to as a "mass layoff event." Eve took no comfort in knowing that she was in the company of 281,500 other laid-off employees across the U.S. when they all filed for unemployment insurance in February. She was the sole support of her nine-year-old son and her widowed mother, and could not afford "an unwanted, unpaid sabbatical." Despite a distinguished career that included dozens of scholarly publications, scores of citations, and many registered patents, she had to face reality: In a down economy, research organizations weren't hiring.

While hunting for a position where she could apply her expertise in systems analysis, Eve started a math tutoring business. The money she made paid for groceries. Rent and her son's private school tuition came straight out of her savings.

Nearly a year passed before Eve was offered two jobs, one with a machine learning start-up in the U.K., the other with a D.C.-based technology integrator serving the U.S. intelligence community. Moving to D.C. was less disruptive for her family so she accepted the position there. Eve's unemployment and her year-long search for stability were so traumatizing that to this day she will not shop at a popular New York mall because it means driving past her former employer's lab.

If the financial crisis of 2008 could rattle a systems analyst trained to work in the well-paying high-tech sector, imagine what it did to the men and women employed in automobile manufacturing, payroll services, food services, temporary help services, and department stores—industries hit hard by the economic crisis.

As brilliant as she was, Eve did not foresee the credit default swap debacle. That's mainly because trouble for middle-class Americans started brewing long before this crisis. In fact, median income for millions of middle-class Americans has been in a long, steady decline since at least the 1990s. Check it out: For 81 percent of counties in the U.S., median income is lower today than it was 15 years ago[1]:

- Meade County, KS, peaked in 2009 at $51,957.
- Worcester County, MA, peaked in 1989 at $67,208.
- Lake County, CA, peaked in 1999 at $41,921.

---

[1] http://www.washingtonpost.com/sf/business/2014/12/12/why-americas-middle-class-is-lost/

- Garfield County, UT, peaked in 1999 at $49,603.
- Franklin County, IA, peaked in 1999 at $50,344.
- Gila County, AZ, peaked in 1969 at $44,567.

How middle-class Americans got left in the lurch is a complicated story, and no two economists will give you the same explanation. Suffice it to say that after the 1990 recession, jobs were slow to reappear. Then came the late nineties tech revolution, which opened up employment possibilities for college grads with a B.A. in everything from accounting to web writing. But when a host of dot-coms, including pets.com, webvan.com, eToys.com and kozmo.com, went belly up, many of the gains associated with the new Internet revolution vanished.

Since the end of the tech bubble, we have lived through two recessions and two so-called "jobless recoveries," a term used to describe macroeconomic growth with steady or decreasing employment. In their aftermath, most Americans discovered they were no better off than they were twenty-five years ago. Even today, when economists and pundits tell us that the financial crisis of 2008 is officially over, we see Americans struggling to live as comfortably as their parents did.

Bob Thompson, a retired aviation factory worker, told *The Washington Post* that his town never regained its footing after the closure of the North American Rockwell plant. These days in Downey, California, Thompson says, "We have a lot of restaurants. There's a lot of minimum wage. People take those jobs."

Thompson, who helped manufacture moon rockets and space shuttles, might well ask, "If we can put a man on the moon, why can't our society come up with good jobs for our people?"

Outsourcing, offshoring, and automation all play a role in having reduced the number and diversity of middle class jobs—and may be indirectly responsible for the ongoing housing crisis. In New York State, for example, new foreclosure cases are being filed at "significantly higher than pre-recession levels," according to an August 2015 New York State comptroller's report. Compare the 47,600 cases filed statewide in 2009 to the 43,900 by 2014. What looks like a modest improvement is actually cause for alarm when you take into account that foreclosure cases had dipped to 16,700 in 2011.

Nationally, though, foreclosures are down. About 549,000 homes were in some stage of foreclosure as of January 2015, down 33.2 percent from 822,000 in January 2014. January 2015 represents thirty-nine consecutive months of year-over-year decline. Absolutely great news. The problem—and mystery, really—is that a stronger housing sector hasn't boosted the economy that much.

This brings us back to the problem we talked about in our chapter on Millennials: Shifts in where people want to live, their capacity to take on debt, and rising construction costs for home builders are keeping middle-class Americans—especially those who traditionally would be buying their first home—from pursuing the dream of home ownership.

The impact on the wider economy can't be ignored. Building a single-family home supports three full-time jobs in construction and ancillary services for a year. Between September 2014 and September 2015, single-family construction amounted to only 1 percent of gross domestic product, approximately half the contribution in the 1990s.

The price per house may be going up, but middle-class Americans can't afford to buy.

It's about income. People just don't have enough of it. The no-money-down programs are gone, too. It's tougher to qualify for a mortgage.

Jenna can tell you just how hard it is to buy a house in a Washington, D.C., suburb. After getting laid off from an advertising job in Manhattan in late 2009, Jenna, 58, made a late-career change and got a Masters in Public Health. Even though she graduated in the top one percent of her class, no healthcare organization in New York or New Jersey ever called her in for an interview. When younger, lower-ranked graduates got job offers, Jenna realized that her age was at least a contributing factor to her unemployment. As a lark, she applied for a job as a clinical research coordinator with a D.C.-based public policy center. Bingo. She accepted their job offer and left her north Jersey suburb for a new life.

After two years in the D.C. area, Jenna is still living in a rental apartment. Her finances have not recovered from her 2009 layoff, her education expenditures, her salary cut, and outlays to help two of her three adult children with their living expenses. Jenna's New Jersey house, which she co-owns with her ex-husband, is on the market. A bid acceptable to them both hasn't materialized.

Because of her loss of income and personal setbacks, Jenna cannot contemplate buying a house in her new community. Zillow's median home value for her D.C. suburb is $359,900, and although home values have declined 3.4 percent over the past year (2015), a down payment and mortgage remain out of reach.

"Show me a single-family home for $350K and I'll show you a leprechaun," Jenna says. "The houses I've looked at are closer to $700K, and I'm not talking about a mansion."

A lot of factors contribute to Jenna's inability to buy a home at this point in her life, but affordability is at the top of the list. A recent Zillow review indicates that someone with a household income of $91,542 could afford a home that costs $415,000. Unfortunately, Jenna hasn't made that salary since she got laid off. At her age, the prospect of making $100,000 ever again is unlikely.

#

If you make between $45,000 and $76,000 a year, the big banks owe you a big thank-you. In 2013 you endowed your J.P. Morgan Chase or Bank of America and other banks in the U.S. with $31.9 billion in overdraft fees. Without your generosity, the big banks would not be able to support their branch-based business model. You should know, too, that this honor belongs entirely to you because banks are not penalizing their wealthy and corporate customers in the same way. So, middle-class America: Here's to you!

The 2010 Dodd-Frank Wall Street Reform and Consumer Protection Act was supposed to curtail a host of banking abuses, including high-to-low transaction processing and automatic over-drafts in the event of insufficient account-holder funds. And yet overdraft fees have crept up from $26 in 2009 to $29 in 2012 to $32.74 in 2014 to $35 in 2015—the seventeenth consecutive record high, according to Bankrate.com. This "creepage" has happened even in the wake of the 2010 legislation that compelled banks to get their customers' consent before charging them fees to cover overdrawn ATM and debit card transactions.

It took J.P. Morgan Chase, Bank of America, and Wells Fargo only the first three months of 2015 to make more than $1.1 billion in overdraft fees. Some 600 other banks tallied up approximately $2.51 billion over the same period of time.

With banking fees in the billions, is it any wonder that all too many middle-class Americans are spending up to 10 percent of their annual income on banking fees alone? And when we say middle class, we mean army veterans who served in Afghanistan as recently as 2014, senior citizens living on a fixed income, blended families struggling to make mortgage payments and fund their children's education, debt-strapped Millennials, and many others.

What your bank does not tell you is just how far they will go to gouge those fees out of you, your parents, your brothers and sisters, your teachers, local firemen, librarians, shop owners, and nearly everyone you come across in your daily life. Here's what you might not know:

- Banks do not properly explain the ceiling and floor on adjustable loans. A floor is the minimum interest rate a bank will charge on a loan; a ceiling is the maximum. The bank will tell you about a special rate on home equity lines of credit and they'll offer you prime minus a quarter. Let's say prime is three and a quarter, but you think you're getting a prime rate of three. Moreover, you think the bank has locked you in at three percent. What the bank hasn't told you is that the floor is four percent, and after a set period of time, say, three months, you'll be charged four percent prime. What about the ceiling? In Pennsylvania, for example, the ceiling is 18 percent. Now, when you're getting a home equity line of credit against your house, you can afford that three or four percent payment. But can you still afford that payment at 18 percent?

- Teaser rates have no written rate guarantee once the teaser period is over. The stated rate on a money market account might be one-and-a-quarter, but the bank won't tell you how long they'll guarantee it. After a short guarantee period, don't be surprised to see the rate plummet.

- Banks grant loan terms that exceed the value of the underlying collateral. This little trick was meant to apply only to car loans (but don't tell that to the anybody whose house in 2008 was worth less than the mortgage owed on it). What happens is you see a car you want for $40,000, but you can't afford to pay off the car loan for four years. What does the bank do? It offers you a loan for five or six years. Now you can afford the car—but there comes a point in that fifth or sixth year when your car is worth less than the amount you owe the bank.

We all want to believe we're too sophisticated to fall for these bank shenanigans. But banks wouldn't invest in them if they didn't work. Free checking almost always pulls us in—until we read the small print. Here is Capital One's disclosure statement about its free checking account: "Like you'd expect from Capital One 360, there are no fees on having your account. But we want to be up front, and let you know that there are six charges you could potentially incur for certain extra services..." The statement goes on to itemize those "extra services" and the fees you will get hit with for using them:

- You pay interest if your balance drops below zero and you use the Overdraft Line of Credit.
- You pay $20 for requesting overnight delivery of a check.
- You pay $25 for overnight delivery of a replacement card.
- You pay a $9.00 "rejected check charge" if you don't have enough funds in your account.
- You pay $25 if you ask the bank to stop payment on a check.

You won't be charged for using your card for a foreign transaction—as long as you notify the bank when you're traveling overseas. (They won't tell you how much they are making on your foreign exchange transfers—it can be up to 20 percent!)

Bank ads are misleading—or outright deceptive—in other less obvious ways, too. For example, let's say that you open up a checking account that gives you 1 percent interest on your first $100,000. Any amount above that and the rate goes down to 25 basis points, or one-quarter percent. Would you assume that you'd actually get a quarter of a percent on the whole balance? Of course not. But that's all you will get if you invest $101,000.

Some more banking fast ones:

- **Clearing checks high to low**. When banks engage in this transaction processing schedule, customers bounce more checks. Here's the galling thing: The banks say they're only trying to help. After all, don't you want your mortgage payment paid before the paperboy? Better to have bad credit with your paperboy than your mortgage lender!

- **Incentive plans and sprints that encourage the wrong behavior toward customers**. A customer comes into the bank for advice on buying or leasing a car. The loan adviser says, "Today is your lucky day. We're running a special on car loans and we've got a great deal for you." What you don't know is that management is pushing an employee incentive plan to sign up car loans. If you had known to ask about leasing or using your home equity line of credit instead, you might have gotten to deduct lease payments or the interest off your taxes. You wanted help. Instead you were sold the "feature of the day."

- **Selling products that are not fully explained**. Our president of community banking told us about an aunt who boasted about investing in a mortgage-backed Ginnie Mae. He said, "Aunt Ruth, I believe in positive thinking, but that's a 30-year instrument. Your principal is guaranteed at the end of 30 years. You're 86. I don't want to be morbid, but the odds aren't good that you're going to live to 116." If her nephew wasn't a banker, Aunt Ruth would have told all her friends to do exactly as she did. And if interest rates were to go up, none of them would ever get all their principal back.

Another friend of our President of Community Banking told him that a big bank in the area convinced her mother to move her money from a money market into a checking account. That meant she was now getting zero percent interest. How did this happen? Because Citizens Bank was rewarding employees for getting customers to open up a checking account.

- **Taking days to notify a customer when they bounce a check**. The goal here is to allow additional bounces—and compounded fees. It goes like this: Most banks are set up to send out non-sufficient funds (NSF) notices by U.S. Mail. If your check bounces at night, the NSF notice is generated, put in an envelope, stamped, and sent out on a Friday. You might not receive it until Monday, while you are at work. The first day you can do anything about your bounced check is Tuesday. By then you will have gotten dinged for three or four days of insufficient funds. Meanwhile, you continue to draw on your account—and continue bouncing other checks.

- **Playing the blind CD rollover game**. You buy a one-year CD. It matures, but you don't need the money right away so you leave your money alone for another year. You assume your money is growing at the same rate. Instead, the banks have dropped the rate dramatically on a one-year CD, and taken advantage of your lack of proactivity If, on the other hand, you're a customer who keeps a close watch on your CD, and you call the bank to close out your CD, the bank can still find a way to take advantage of you. It may offer you an 11-month CD with a lower maturity rate than that of your one-year CD. And you figure, "Why not. I'll take it." The banks take advantage of their customers in this way all the time.

- **Selling products that are better for the bank than the customer**. When a bank pushes a particular product—say, a non-FDIC-insured investment—you have to ask yourself who benefits. More likely than not, it's the bank employee who has been incentivized to push it.

- **Engaging in malpractice**. You come into the bank and ask to open a $10,000 CD. You may not know that the bank is actually pushing $10,000 CDs and your banker will open one for you, no questions asked. How is that different from your coming into a doctor's office with a sore throat and asking for penicillin? A good doctor will take the time to assess what your problem is and what medication is right for you. A good banker should understand what you are trying to achieve and provide you with solutions that are good for you.

So much chicanery. Why?

Because the banks are striking back. At what?

At Dodd-Frank. It was designed to stop banks from gambling with your money.

But that's a good thing, isn't it?

For you, the provisions of Dodd-Frank are beneficial. For the banks— not so much. In December 2014, banks actually lobbied Congress to rescind the Dodd-Frank rule that bars insured institutions (that is, banks) from dealing in exotic securities. Why did they want the right to go back into the casino? They argued that they need to look for more ways to make up for lost revenue. That explains why the credit default swap, which rained down so much misery on mortgage holders, is making its way back.

The bizarre thing is that you are getting chiseled in an age when technology could help you save money, insure the safety of your deposits, facilitate financial advice, and improve your quality of life.

You're being shortchanged in an era when big data analytics are helping big organizations and individuals alike maximize their savings. Banks already have a lot of data about you. They could be using it to analyze your transaction data and help you understand your spending habits. If necessary, they could show you how to get them under control.

In the best of all possible worlds, your bank would serve as a financial advisor. Say, you're in the market for a new car. At the car lot, you take a photo of the car you like and text it to your banker. Your banker quotes the car's wholesale price and compares it to the manufacturer's suggested price. He or she advises you about financing it over the next 48 months, compared to what it would cost if you leased it.

You'd have pretty much the same scenario when you're in the market for a house. You'd take a photo and text it over to your bank, which then comes up with the appraised value of the house. Based on the zip code, your bank tells you what the average interest rates are for a 15-year and 30-year fixed mortgage. Your bank knows if you can afford the payment or not.

The purpose of a bank isn't only to lend you money and accept your money as deposits. It's also to give you information you can use. The purpose of a bank is to help you, your family, and your small business succeed. It certainly isn't to smack you over the head with a bunch of nuisance fees.

Your bank should treat you the same way they treat a millionaire. They can't, though, because banks live off of the fees generated by basic checking account holders like you.

You may be too young to remember that banks once gave out a free toaster for opening up a checking account. Why did they do that?

Because the kind of person who wanted a freebie was the kind of person likely to run up a debt. The era of free toasters is long gone because banks now rely on fees—arguably a better way of making money off of you.

Banks would do a lot better to understand their customers, the way, say, Apple does, or Amazon, Netflix, Facebook, Uber, and Pandora. Those companies work hard to understand consumers' needs and preferences. Banks, on the other hand, are intentionally blind to the reality of your life. They don't want to understand that if you're married and have one or two children, you have to think about funding their education. You think twice before buying a home or a car.

If you're a member of the middle class, you have unique problems related to your stage in life and your short- and long-term goals. But instead of helping you solve your individual problems, banks tend to offer a one-size-fits-all solution. If they truly cared about their middle-class customers, they would combine "customization" and digital technology and put you—not their branch offices—at the center of their business model.

No other industry is as tone-deaf as banking. Travel, hospitality, publishing, retail, and computing have turned themselves upside down and inside out to give their customers what they want.

The banking industry is clueless.

Every other industry conducts market research to understand their customers' needs and innovate to meet those needs.

Banking turns a blind eye.

The banks may not care, but various organizations have studied how middle-class Americans feel about themselves and their prospects:

- **Pew Research Report.** The Washington, D.C.-based think tank reported in January 2014 that 44 percent of American adults identify themselves as middle class. Compare that to the same survey conducted in 2008, during the first months of the Great Recession, when 53 percent called themselves middle class.

- **Gallup, Inc.** In April 2015, the Washington, D.C.-based performance management consulting company reported that 51 percent of Americans call themselves middle or upper-middle class; 48 percent say they are lower or working class. In multiple surveys conducted between 2000 and 2008, approximately 60 percent of Americans identified themselves as middle or upper-middle class.

- **Bureau of Labor Statistics.** In August 2015, the BLS reported that 77.2 percent of all 25-to-54-year-olds were employed. This figure is significantly below the pre-recession (October 2006) employment-to-population ratio, when 80.7 percent of people in this age group were employed. Relatively speaking, middle-class employment is down even as bank fees become more consistent—and more punitive.

- **The COUNTRY Financial Security Index**. In a May 2015 survey of Americans' attitudes toward finances, COUNTRY reported "increased levels of confidence in all areas of money management, including their ability to save, invest, retire, and pay off debts." Yet only 18 percent of Americans say they are "very confident" that they can afford to send their children to college.

In light of this depressing data, what are banks doing to help their middle-class customers?

They're exhausting you with fees.

Banks have forgotten that their mission is to accelerate the flow of money: for individuals, families, and small businesses. It's tragic. With mobile technology, banking can be as digital—and as affordable—as Fandango, PayPal, or Uber. It can recreate the branch experience on your smartphone or tablet, so you can open a checking account, pay your bills, send money to your family or friends, invest, qualify for a loan, or talk to a financial advisor without ever walking into a branch.

The bank that is ready, willing, and able to use technology to help middle-class Americans prosper is the bank that will restore people's confidence in our economic system.

And on that note, banks of America, we'd like a word with you.

The middle class, small business, and the Millennials are waiting—but not necessarily for you. They are already investigating alternative ways to pay their bills: Venmo, PayPal, Google Wallet, WePay, 2Checkout, authorize.Net, Skrill, Intuit, ProPay, Click2Sell,

Dwolla, Braintree, ClickBank, and Stripe. If you want to be a partner to the people who need banking services, you will have to help them pay their bills, save money, facilitate home ownership in a way that is fair and responsible, and help them repay their college loans. Because if you think your century-old approach to banking is going to keep working for you and your unhappy middle-class customers, just ask Borders Bookstores, Blockbuster, Tower Records, Encyclopedia Britannica, the United States Postal Service, Kodak, and Circuit City what they would do if they had it to do all over again.

CHAPTER 5

What the Underbanked and Unbanked Want from Their Bank

ELSIE, 51, IS NOT PROUD OF THE WAY SHE ONCE DEALT with her money problems.

Her story begins in Yonkers, New York, where she was living with her twin boys and two daughters. Her sons, both high-achieving students and athletes, were gunned down in their teens in separate incidents. Elsie had been looking forward to their high school graduation, when they planned on opening a carpentry and furniture restoration workshop. "I was counting on them to help out with the mortgage," she says.

Elsie worked as an administrative assistant through a secretarial temping service. Occasionally, she landed a regular nine-to-five job, often with a medium- or large-sized company, but more typically, she settled for month-long stints when female employees were out on maternity leave. She readily admits that the obstacle to a steady job with benefits was lack of education. "My dream was to get certified as a phlebotomist, but everything I earned went to the mortgage and our daily expenses," Elsie says.

Elsie's longest temp job was with a global insurance company in midtown Manhattan. "My manager tried to warn me that my skills were out of date," she says. "He advised me to learn programs like Photoshop and Excel. But I was waiting for my girls to graduate so I could apply for a phlebotomy program. I know now I was wrong to put all my eggs in one basket, especially because our local high school was offering Photoshop and Excel [classes] on Saturdays for free."

The temp jobs for a fortysomething woman with obsolete office skills dried up. Elsie tried to find work as a babysitter or housecleaner, but younger women got hired ahead of her. For the first time in her adult life, Elsie was in danger of missing a mortgage payment.

"I couldn't even take out a payday loan because I wasn't working," she says.

Elsie says it took all her nerve to ask an account manager she knew at the insurance company for five hundred dollars.

"I had a strategy," she says. "I would ask for five hundred and repay it. The next time I'd ask for more and ..." Elsie had no intention of repaying the bigger loan. She let her mortgage go into arrears and moved with her children to Smyrna, Georgia, where her sister was willing to let her stay until she got back on her feet.

Elsie concedes that she left a lot of "wreckage" behind in Yonkers. "I didn't just run out on my mortgage," she says. "I didn't pay my utilities bill, my phone bill, or the purchases I put on my three credit cards."

Elsie regrets not having moved in with her sister before her financial situation unraveled. With a loan from her sister, she was able to enroll in a phlebotomy certificate program at a Marietta, Georgia, medical training center. Within three months, Elsie passed the national certification test. Thanks to a recommendation from one of her instructors, she found a position with a small family practice in Smyrna, a fifteen-minute walk from her sister's house. Her starting salary was $30,200—not a princely sum, but Elsie was able to save up enough money to rent a two-bedroom apartment in Smyrna.

As for the "wreckage" Elsie left behind in Yonkers: Her lender repossessed the house and resold it within six months at an auction. Her credit score dropped 300 points and she will not be eligible for a Fannie Mae mortgage for seven years. As for a deficiency judgment of $1,200 that the New York court system lodged against Elsie, she has paid off half of it.

After six months on the job, Elsie opened a checking account at a local state bank. She chose the no-interest account because of the terms: Only $100 was required to open the account and there were no minimum balances, monthly service charges, or per check fees. She began working with a debt consolidation counseling service in early 2015 to start chipping away at her $6,000 in credit card debt.

"Some pay periods I only save ten dollars," Elsie says. "But I was never so proud of saving ten dollars in my life."

#

The 9.6 million unbanked (11 percent of all banking consumers) and the 24 million underbanked (17 percent) are not exactly rarities in American life. In fact, the FDIC believes the number of underbanked could actually be as high as 60 million. More than a third of unbanked households entered this club after a job loss or some other significant drop in income. About the same percentage of unbanked households report they simply do not have enough money to keep in an account or meet minimum balance requirements.

When we talk about the unbanked and underbanked, we mean people, like Elsie, with limited financial resources. Up until ten or fifteen years ago, we called them poor. More and more, though, people who do not have banking services are what we once called middle class: the pipe fitters and clerks whose $40,000-a-year income was sufficient to start a family and make a down payment on a house. In many states today, $40K qualifies you for charity care at a hospital.

The unbanked and underbanked might be you. Your parents. Your children. Your friends.

A lot of factors have contributed to the dismemberment of the middle class. This is not the place to analyze them at length, but we do want to identify four things that have contributed to this terrible situation: (1) the fallout from the 2008 banking crisis; (2) the offshoring of jobs in the manufacturing and service sectors; (3) the use of automation to replace manual jobs, and (4) the stagnation of wages. Indeed, Census Bureau data confirm that America's middle class is still struggling to recover from the Great Recession and decades of sluggish economic growth.

We bring up the middle class again to emphasize the fact that many of the unbanked and underbanked were once part of it. Or had a shot at joining it.

We bring it up to insist that the banks—which contributed overwhelmingly to the financial crisis of 2008—have an obligation to restore working Americans to a financial condition that will let them pay off their debt and save money.

The banks should be helping in two ways:

- They should not be making matters worse by turning a blind eye to the unbanked and underbanked.
- They should be helping people participate in the economy, not simply struggle to hold onto its coattails.

Microsoft cofounder Bill Gates understands the seriousness of the problem on a macro scale. His Gates Foundation has reported that more than 2.5 billion adults around the world do not have a checking account at any financial institution. Like their unbanked counterparts in the developed world, poor households rely on informal providers—money lenders of one sort or another. And as with payday lenders, mechanisms outside the formal banking system inevitably suck borrowers into a downward spiral of high interest rates and chronic debt.

Gates has always been a proponent of the right technology at the right time. He knows that the brick-and-mortar banking system can't lift people out of poverty, largely because the poor conduct their transactions in cash, but also because banks aren't using the right technology. Processing cash transactions is relatively expensive for banks, utility companies, and other businesses, which pass along the costs associated with storing, transporting, and processing cash to us. With digital payment systems, though, storing and transferring money is instantaneous—and advantageous: Mobile financial platforms can connect poor households to affordable and reliable financial tools through phones, kiosks, and other digital interfaces.

How do we know this is possible?

Because, of the 2.5 billion people in the world without access to a traditional bank, approximately one billion have a mobile phone.

The Gates Foundation believes that in addition to cost savings, digital services offer a way for:

- Poor people to become customers and suppliers within the wider economy.
- Customers to keep track of financial flows, resulting in safer and speedier transactions (as well as fewer opportunities for corruption and theft).
- Financial providers to develop products (including fee-for-service offerings and micro-transactions) better suited to customers' needs and capacity for risk.
- Workers and citizens to benefit from direct deposits (wages and government assistance), which often give women greater financial authority within the family.
- Banks to inform customers about upcoming bills and affordable financial products.

Bill Gates predicts that by 2030, some two billion people will enter into the formal financial system, thanks to mobile technologies. That may be why he has committed millions of his foundation's money to get the global unbanked started with affordable checking accounts.

We need a Gates-like plan for America.

#

We do not have to tell you that the unbanked and underbanked in our own country do not have many sustainable options. If you don't have a checking account, you may resort to alternative financial services such as payday lenders, prepaid debit cards, and pawn shops. These are all spit-and-chewing gum solutions that have sprung up to fill the void left by a mainstream banking system that's not designed to serve the most financially fragile Americans.

The Board of Governors of the Federal Reserve System will be the first to tell you that alternative financial services, known for their high interest rates and service charges (i.e., fees), are a costly way of managing household finances if not used carefully. Worst of all, these "alternatives" promise consumers few regulatory protections.

Here's a look at some of the current alternative financial services options:

- **Prepaid cards.** If you can't open a checking account because you have mismanaged your finances, or because you're unemployed, or because you are living paycheck to paycheck, you might buy a prepaid card. The plus is that you can reload cash onto these cards at CVS, Walmart, and other big-box stores. Some prepaid cards even let you use ATMs for free.

But watch out for the fees! In monthly charges alone, a typical prepaid card will hit you up for approximately $300 a year. This figure doesn't include activation fees, transaction fees, bill payment fees, declined transaction fees, inactivity fees, customer service fees, and paper statement fees. And if the issuing financial entity isn't FDIC-insured, you'll probably lose the balance of your card if the company fails.

- **Payday loans**. These are cash advances for relatively small amounts of money that you have to repay on your next payday or in installments over a set period of time. You might receive the funds via cash or check, a prepaid debit card, or an e-transfer into your bank account. Finance charges range from $10 to $30 for every $100 borrowed. Think of it this way: A two-week loan for $100 with a $15 fee represents an annual percentage rate (APR) of almost 400 percent.

Payday lenders—companies that loan you small amounts of money at high interest rates and expect you to repay with your next paycheck—make up a $46 billion-a-year business. In 2012, the year for which we have the most recent figures, $3.4-$4.5 billion of that amount came from fee payments. To appreciate the toll that payday loans take on the borrower, a $300 loan might actually be worth only $255 after you subtract $45 for fees. If you take out ten small payday loans, you'll owe $450 in fees. It's not for nothing that the U.S. Consumer Financial Protection Bureau calls payday loans "debt traps."

The industry has grown fast. In twenty years, the number of payday loan stores in the U.S. has outstripped the number of Starbucks and McDonald's. Political comedian John Oliver has said that the Ebola virus looks at that growth rate and says, "That's impressive! You guys spread fast!"

Who uses payday loans?

Most payday loan recipients are white, female, and between the ages of 25 and 44.

They are also predominantly:
- Without a four-year college degree.
- Home renters.
- African Americans.
- Earning less than $40,000 a year.
- Separated or divorced.

All told, 12 million Americans spend upwards of seven billion dollars a year on payday loans. A typical borrower takes out eight loans of $375 each per year—for a total of $3,000—and spends $520 on interest.

Why do people saddle themselves with payday loans?

Sixty-nine percent of borrowers need money to cover ordinary monthly living expenses: utilities, rent, food, mortgage payments, or credit card bills.

Sixteen percent of borrowers have unexpected expenses: a car repair or an emergency medical issue.

The Pew Charitable Trusts, a think tank that studied payday lending in America (2012), reported that just under half of all American families are "income-constrained." That means their household expenditures are higher than their income. Eight percent are "debt-challenged," meaning that they spend 41 percent or more of their gross monthly income to pay off their debt. Sometimes they borrow from retirement accounts or prematurely sell off investments. Not surprisingly, the average borrower is in debt about five months of the year.

The majority of payday borrowers are unbanked—they don't have a checking account—or underbanked—they have a checking account but no access to any other financial services. The big problem with payday loans (sometimes called check cashing) is the lender's exorbitant fees. Regions Bank charges between 1.5 and 3 percent of the check, plus a minimum fee of three dollars. Ace Cash Express charges 3 percent of the check amount. Walmart charges $3 to cash checks of $1,000 or less and $6 for checks of $1,001 to $5,000. In New York State, the annual percentage rate for a fourteen-day loan is between 200 and 500 percent.

As if racking up compounded debt wasn't enough, payday borrowers tell nightmare stories about lenders who threaten to put them in jail, take away their children, dig up dead relatives, or kill pets. Hackers have gotten into payday lender websites, stolen customer data, and then disguised themselves as debt collectors. These Dickensian tales of financial abuse have become so commonplace that in March 2015, the Consumer Financial Protection Bureau (CFPB) proposed regulations that would rein in payday loans with interest rates of 400 percent or more.

These regulations, however, will not ban the high-interest, short-term loans that people take out to cover basic expenses. They will merely require lenders to assess a borrower's income, other financial obligations, and borrowing history to insure that when the loan comes due, the borrower will be able to pay back the loan. Alternatively, the lender would have to limit loans to $500. If this is the case, the lender could not roll over loans more than two times during a twelve-month period.

The CFPB came up with these regulations after analyzing fifteen million payday loans. The consumer bureau learned that borrowers took out a median of ten loans during a twelve-month span. Borrowers who took out eleven or more loans account for 75 percent of payday loan fees.

(John Oliver says payday loans are the Lay's Potato Chips of finance. You can't have just one—and they're terrible for you.)

Until 2015, payday lending had been largely regulated by the states. North Carolina military officials in late 2014, for example, denounced state legislation that would permit payday lenders to increase their fees or interest rates for young soldiers, some of them fresh out of high school. An acting senior commander at Fort Bragg worried that national security would be at risk if the state bill passed and permitted lenders to make larger installment loans at the highest permissible rate. Another commander said that "out-of-control debt" could jeopardize soldiers' security clearances.

Payday lenders say they had to increase fees or interest rates for subpar creditors, like U.S. soldiers, in order to finance their branch offices and hire employees. Meanwhile, OneMain Financial, a payday unit of Citigroup, reported an increase in profits of 31 percent between 2012 and 2013.

Lest you think that mobile technology—without risk management and fiduciary oversight—will cure all ills, a 2014 Pew report found that one in three borrowers signed on for loans that renewed automatically. Forty-six percent of online borrowers reported that a lender made withdrawals that overdrew their checking accounts. Thirty percent said that a lender or debt collector had threatened them. And at 650 percent annual percentage rate (APR), online payday loans are actually more expensive to use than a brick-and-mortar store. Pew's conclusion: Payday loans, whether online or storefront, "fail to work as advertised."

Here's the problem with using payday loans.

Say you are making less than $52,000 a year. If you resort to one of these loans, you are spending 10 percent of your income outside the banking system. This amounts to a 10 percent poverty tax simply because you are low income. Shadow banking operations, which also includes prepaid debit cards, are chipping away at a banking industry that is not serving low-income people, the middle class, or Millennials. The government may end up regulating payday lenders and prepaid debit card companies, but that may simply mean that they have to offer more transparent information about fees. Increased transparency will do for the payday lending industry what the Surgeon General's warning did for the tobacco industry: It'll let them off the hook.

The 29 percent of the U.S. population that makes less than $52,000 a year needs a way to hold onto the 10 percent "poverty tax" they are paying out to alternative financial systems. If our country intends to climb out of the 2008 financial crisis and continue to prosper, we need to insure that a third of the country pockets more of their own money. As long as the payday lending industry is making $4 billion a year on the unbanked and underbanked, we'll end up with a rich economy full of desperately poor people. And the major banks will have only themselves to blame, because they own many of the biggest payday loan companies, thus perpetuating the cycle.

The federal government has sought to intervene, with limited success. In fact, the United States has been much more successful at bringing banking to poor people across the planet than across the fifty states. According to the *Financial Times*, more than 700 million people have received access to banking in the last three years[1] This reduces the risk they face when carrying cash from their jobs in the cities to the villages where their families reside. At the same time, however, 25 million American adults lack access to banking services. So the question is, how can the U.S. government provide banking services for its citizens?

The challenge is that banks' high minimum balances and fee structures drive the poor from using traditional banks and force them into the arms of payday lenders. Those lenders charge even higher fees and do not encourage saving. According to the *Financial Times* report, almost 58 percent of unbanked households said they

---

[1] *The Financial Times*, November 30, 2015, "US tries to boost access to 25m 'unbanked'": http://www.ft.com/intl/cms/s/0/6fc33f02-9785-11e5-95c7-d47aa298f769.html

lacked enough money to meet minimum balances, and a third of those households blamed high or unpredictable fees. The federal government has been working with banks to reduce fees for low-income customers.

Why would anybody take out a payday loan? If you're living on the financial margins, you know you're going to have a rough time getting a bank loan or a credit card. And if you think the government is the only thing standing between you and the predatory tactics of payday lenders, you should know that beginning in 2012, state legislatures voted to *increase* the fees or interest rates that lenders to subpar borrowers can charge. Subprime consumer lenders such as Citigroup's OneMain Financial argued successfully that they had to raise rates because—you guessed it—they have to keep up with the cost of running their branches.

Well, everything is relative, so maybe a payday loan feels easier to deal with than Citigroup's "bad bank" unit, which charges its 1.3 million customers interest rates of up to 36 percent.

It's not. In an August 2014 indictment, Manhattan district attorney Cyrus R. Vance, Jr., said that the payday industry's "exorbitant interest rates and automatic payments from borrowers' bank accounts are sadly typical of this industry as a whole." Vance's indictment went on to call one Tennessee-based payday lender a "syndicate" that controlled every aspect of the loan process: extending the loans, processing payments, and collecting from borrowers behind on their bills. Vance called it: The payday lender's goal is to make expensive loans even in a state like Tennessee, that outlaws them.

This particular lender got around Tennessee's payday regulations by incorporating its online payday lending arm beyond the reach of American prosecution—in the West Indies. It operated a network of individual companies responsible for specific lending functions, such as loan applications, loan approvals, and loan collections from borrowers. By setting up shop across the country, this lender avoided interest rate caps in fifteen states. So, even though New York has a usury law cap of 25 percent per loan, the lender charged borrowers between 350 and 650 percent simply by originating the loans in other states.

Some good news for payday borrowers came in February 2015, when the Consumer Financial Protection Bureau (CFPB) announced it would release the first draft of federal regulations that would govern a wide range of short-term loans.

The bad news: Payday lenders are already looking to exploit a loophole in a rule that lets lenders make six unaffordable loans a year.

Why not close up these loopholes?

The CFPB was pressured by Congress and financial industry groups to strike a "precarious balance" so it could eliminate most predatory loans without choking off credit "options" for poor consumers.

What the "legit" subprime and alternative payday lenders have in common is a fee-based strategy to make money off of people who are either outside the banking system or just peripherally connected to it. The payday lending industry's 22,000 payday locations generated $27 billion in 2012, and Citigroup's OneMain Financial held $8.1 billion of loans as of June 30, 2014. Oh, and four months later it filed for an initial public offering (IPO) expected to raise one billion dollars.

Sweet, but probably not for you.

- **Pawn shops**. Contrary to the Hollywood image of a dingy backstreet store that buys and sells used guns, jewelry, and musical instruments, a pawn shop is licensed by state and local government to offer customers a loan. In exchange for a loan, you have to offer some valuable item as collateral. The pawnbroker gives you a fixed amount of time to pay the loan back with interest. If you don't repay the loan in time, the pawn shop has the right to resell your valuable item.

  The problem here too is stratospheric interest rates. You'll be told that the annual interest rate on a $200 loan is, say, 29 percent. But when you return in a month to repay it, you will be charged the full 29 percent and pay $258.00. The annual rate on this loan is actually 348 percent. Pawnbroking may be a regulated industry, but who benefits from regulated extortion? Not you.

If banks have failed the 29 percent of Americans who have a tenuous hold on the banking system—or none at all—why blame the debit card and payday companies for rushing in to fill the void? All they're doing is providing a service for an unmet economic and social need, aren't they?

You can only get behind this kind of cynical thinking if you don't accept the role that banking plays in a high-functioning capitalist society.

Banking is how society regulates its economy in a way that avoids chaos and fear. So critical is this premise that any group that wants to manage cash, loans, and credit has to acquire a bank charter from the Federal Deposit Insurance Corporation (FDIC) and then submit to regulation by the Office of the Comptroller of the Currency. The OCC's mission is plain: "To ensure that national banks and federal savings associations operate in a safe and sound manner, provide fair access to financial services, treat customers fairly, and comply with applicable laws and regulations."

None of the businesses offering prepaid debit cards and payday loans—the shadow banking enterprises—have bank charters. Not that they need them. Only entities that accept traditional bank deposits have to have a charter. Organizations that facilitate credit are not subject to the same regulatory oversight.

How convenient!

#

We want to give a shout-out to 7-Eleven, the Japanese-owned convenience franchise whose consumer base—in Japan and the U.S.—consists predominantly of the unbanked and underbanked. Japanese customers, who often don't own credit cards, visit 7-Eleven to pay for bills and purchases with cash. The needs of cash-based U.S. consumers, however, have gone mostly ignored. To stay competitive, 7-Eleven recognized that it had to find a way to serve its U.S. customers without also incurring prohibitive costs associated with cash transactions.

The franchise partnered with PayNearMe, a digital payment system that enables cash payments for online purchases, utilities, and rent. Since September 2010, 6,200 U.S. 7-Eleven stores have made cash payments possible by letting customers use their smartphones to open up an account they can use to pay their bills and make online and in-store purchases.

Thanks to a recent update to the 7-Eleven Bill Pay app, customers can now pay their bills, keep track of their payment history and past receipts, and set reminders to make their monthly payments.

The 7-Eleven franchise is effectively accommodating its unbanked and underbanked customers *and* staying competitive. It accomplished these two objectives by thinking like a software company *and* a retail store. The most innovative banks and financial systems are all doing just that—outside the U.S.

In New Zealand, Westpac Bank's chief digital officer leveraged the data analytics capabilities of IBM Watson Explorer to develop Westpac One, a device-neutral platform that emphasizes customer experience over whiz-bang technology. "We had to fundamentally change the way we thought and the way we worked," says chief digital officer Simon Pomeroy, who insists that the biggest barrier to creating a seamless banking experience across all channels—online, branch, and call center—was "ourselves."

Westpac One lets customers perform some 120 functions on a smartphone, tablet, or computer, everything from transferring money between accounts to getting preliminary approvals on mortgage applications. From the customer's standpoint, the greatest achievement is that all customer data appears on a single screen: checking and savings account info, mortgage, credit cards, retirement funds, etc. Westpac created an exciting banking experience because it went the distance to understand its customers.

"We want to simplify and automate what I'll call most of our low-value but high-volume transactions," says CDO Pomeroy. "And that will enable us to free up our people to be able to have more engaging, advisory conversations with customers. And that conversation can happen through chat. It can happen through a remote face-to-face conversation or it can happen face-to-face in a branch. It really will depend on the customer's preference as to how they want to have that conversation."

How's it all working out for Westpac?

Three years ago, the bank was interacting with fewer than 40 percent of its customers, and most of those conversations were reactive. In 2014 it interacted with more than 92 percent of them—and most of these conversations were the result of proactive engagements.

Westpac One sounds like an incredible system. With the ability to service low-value, high-volume transactions at relatively low cost, it stands to revolutionize the lives of unbanked and underbanked New Zealanders.

#

Back to the person—like you—who might be making $40,000 a year and spending ten percent of it on shadow banking services.

You need a bank where your money is safe and secure. It's not safe in an alternative, predatory system that has rolled in like a toxic cloud to exploit your poverty. The only foreseeable hope is the device you've got in your hands: your mobile phone. Some 69 percent of the unbanked and 88 percent of the underbanked are using mobile devices. If the banks want to get serious about reinvigorating the economy and letting you hold onto more of your own money, they have to come up with innovative mobile banking solutions.

Fast.

Like Westpac. Like Bankmobile. Ready to help you deposit your money safely, offer financial advice, and improve the quality of your everyday life. Ready to make you say, "Wow! I finally found a transparent, effortless bank!"

Bankmobile won't be the first FDIC-insured mobile bank on the market, but we'll be the first to tell it like it is: The current state of affairs in the banking industry—the overdraft fees, the checking account balance fees, the astronomical interest rates on credit, and the dishonest sales practices, is gutting the middle class and crippling the poor. Only FDIC-insured mobile banking can help you become secure enough to save and make more money. You can pay fees and let banks stay inefficient and principally serve the wealthy and big business. Or you can help start a banking revolution and start your first fee free banking experience with us.

You don't have to let the banks and alternative cash companies beat you up anymore. You've got a smart device. You're already halfway to your own financial recovery.

CHAPTER 6

How to Use Your Bank to Your Best Advantage

JAY: IF YOU HAVE PAID OVERDRAFT FEES OR ARE PAYING monthly fees for checking accounts or prepaid cards; if you don't have a checking account because you can't afford one; if you're stressed out because you were laid off and haven't yet found work that pays as much as your last job; or if a major life event—divorce or widowhood—has destabilized your finances, please do not think that I am light years removed from your problems. I've made good money in my life, but I've also lost a lot of money. Using my own financial ups and downs as a starting point, I want to talk to you about some basic but crucial strategies and tactics you can use to get the most out of your bank.

Let's start by talking about:
- Saving your money
- Managing your loans and debt

- Planning for major life events
- Investing your money
- Setting money aside for taxes

SAVING YOUR MONEY

Rule #1. Whether you're making $40,000 or $140,000 a year, slice five-to-ten percent off your paycheck every month and put it into a high-rate savings account where you can't easily get at it. A company-matched 401(k) is an excellent lock box for this money: If you touch it for any purpose other than retirement, you'll get smacked with a financial penalty. Depending on your 401(k) investments, you can increase your savings 20, even 50 percent over the lifetime of your employment. If you invest in an index fund that increases your account 15 percent on average, you can almost double your money every five years. Of course you'll add to that index fund every pay period. And thanks to the power of compounding, your savings will increase manifold.

Einstein supposedly said, "Compound interest is the eighth wonder of the world. He who understands it, earns it. He who doesn't, pays it." That's smart, even if it's apocryphal.

Rule #2. Set up a Rainy Day Fund equal to at least one paycheck. Fixing a flat tire, for example, should not send you to the poorhouse. Whatever the unforeseen event—a pet in need of a visit to the vet, a flooded basement, a fuel surcharge on your rent—it will find you. Be prepared for it.

Rule #3. Watch your pennies. The grande caffe mocha at Starbucks ($4.15) you toss back for your morning fuel costs a few pennies more than the large cappuccino at Dunkin' Donuts ($3.49) and the large McCafe mocha at McDonald's ($3.39). True, we're talking about a difference of only 66 cents and 76 cents, respectively. But 66 cents five days a week amounts to $3.30 a week, and 76 cents means $3.80 a week. By choosing the cheaper option, you can save between $171.60 and $197.60 a year, respectively.

Not worth forgoing the pleasure? Think about all your other discretionary expenses: getting together with friends for drinks, eating out or eating take-out, smoking cigarettes. You're looking at hundreds, quite possibly thousands, more dollars you could be saving.

We're not saying you should live like a monk. We're advocating for a money-conscious lifestyle, wherever you fall on the earnings scale. If you're really hooked on your morning joe, look for coupons or store cards that will reward you with one free cup for every ten purchases. Make Groupon and other discounters a way of life. It doesn't matter what you're looking for—$30 worth of humanely raised, hormone-free local beef for $22 or a $200 online Microsoft Excel certification course for $19—you'll find it and other deals to enhance your life.

Always be looking to save money. Recently, I had a choice between taking the 2:00 or 2:02 from Washington, D.C. to New York City. The 2:02 cost 50 percent less than the 2:00 and would arrive in NYC fourteen minutes later. It made no sense to take the more expensive train when it would get me to my destination at almost the same time. I saved $123. I like that kind of reward.

The entire BankMobile team travels coach. Our CFO tells me that at a previous job, he always traveled business class. We've told him that being money-conscious is a mindset. None of us travel business class and none of us eat in an executive dining room. Would it "break the bank" for us to splurge on travel and food? No, but who'd be paying for those indulgences? Our customers. We could afford all kinds of perks, but we're committed to a watch-your-pennies culture.

Personally speaking, I book my hotels and car rentals through Hotwire or Priceline because they give me the option of bidding. It's amazing that you can bid $8 for a $35 car—and 50 percent of the time, you'll win. For the extra two minutes it takes to get the better deal, I save $1,000 a year in business travel.

Vacation travel bargains can save you money, too. A search on Travelocity from Newark Airport to Cancun, Mexico, for example, turns up airfare-hotel deals that range between $696 per person (walking distance to the beach) and $2,607 (beachfront). An Orbitz search for the same trip yields a stay at the beachfront Westin Resort & Spa for $916 per person or $2,286 at the Fiesta Americana Condesa. Clearly, these deals may not be of equal value in terms of accommodations, view, beach access, shopping, and proximity to tourist sites. But if all you want is a week of snorkeling, you shouldn't pay for access to shopping and tourist sites.

A little Googling will save you money that you can put away for a rainy day. And you won't be paying for extras you don't want. So will a search for "travel apps" on your smartphone: TripAdvisor, Kayak Flights, Expedia Hotels & Flights, Orbitz, Hotels Tonight, Booking.com and Skyscanner, to name a handful. They're all free downloads.

Don't forget to look at travel blogs and online newspaper columns. We follow Seth Kugel, the "Frugal Traveler," at NYTimes. com, but a lot of others are worth investigating, too, including 12hrs, Melting Butter, EatingAsia, Sidetracked, Feather and Flip, and The American Guide.

Rule #4. Think rich but live frugal. The most famous avatar of this principle is Warren Buffett. The man is blessed with a near-indifference to material wealth. He reportedly still lives in the house he bought in 1958 for $31,500. He admits to liking nothing better than running Berkshire Hathaway, his Omaha, Nebraska-based holding company that owns GEICO, Dairy Queen, and Fruit of the Loom, to name a few, and has significant minority ownership in American Express, Wells Fargo, and IBM, among others. He is said to spend his free time watching sports on TV.

We have a millionaire friend named Michael who is the incarnation of the Buffett mindset. He has never bought a pen for his business. "I pick them up at the conferences I attend," he says. "If I already own them, I don't have to buy them."

Rule #5. Treat your employer's money as if it were your own. Throughout our working lives, we've all encountered people who are workplace spoiled brats. They learn how to talk the talk, but secretly they always feel entitled to get a little bit more: the extra drink they put on the company expense account, the reams of copy paper they slip into their briefcase, the sick day they take to go skiing. Don't be a faker. As smart as you think you are, you can't mask a sense of entitlement for long. Eventually, employers will see through it. A savvy employer will reward sincere commitment and show the blowhard the door.

Many years ago, a story surfaced in the media about an executive caught on video scraping the wall of a company hallway with his coin. Despite the work he had put into his career, and despite the advantages he had enjoyed, he had some kind of "Dr. Jekyll and Mr. Hyde" split personality about his employer. Maybe he should have seen a therapist. Everything this man had achieved was undone in one childish display of pique caught on a security camera. Don't be this guy.

If you want a role model, be Sam Walton, the late founder and CEO of Walmart. It's said that, in spite of his vast wealth, he used to turn the lights off whenever he left a room. Did his energy-saving habit enrich Walmart? Probably not. What they did do, though, was establish a mindset. It says every employee should look upon the company as his own personal asset. And that when it comes to caring about the company every day in every way, the CEO is no different than the store greeter.

Workplace success—and more money—will come to those who genuinely follow this rule.

Rule #6. Never—ever—pay outrageous nuisance fees. Let's face it. Some people get ahead by ripping other people off. Exploitation and disrespect become a way of life. They will keep exploiting and disrespecting the schmo who is weak enough to let them get away with it. All you can do is stay true to a fair and responsible way of life.

So, if you forget to pay your credit card or if you make a mistake and you overdraw your checking account, pick up the phone. Call your credit card issuer. Call your bank. Tell them you made an honest mistake. Nine times out of ten, you will talk to somebody who will sympathize and reverse the fee.

If you do end up dealing with the ripoff artist, consider it a lesson learned. That's what a friend of ours did after he put $500,000 of his money in a Chase retirement account. It sat there for sixty days while he waited for a stock he had his eye on to reach his desired share price. In that time, Chase paid him $3 interest and charged him $35 for having an inactive cash account. Can you believe it? A wealthy client had half a million dollars with this bank and the bank's attitude was, "Sorry, these are our fees."

It's galling enough when a bank rips off a high-net-worth client. But it's much more terrible when you have a precious $3,500 to put into a retirement account and the bank charges you $35 because its "inactive," or for some other infraction buried in their fine print.. Some banks get rich by charging fees that in any other situation would simply be illegal.

There are a few bank fees you can nearly always avoid, including the out-of-network ATM fee, which has gone up to $5 or more per transaction in New York City and Atlanta, while remaining a "bargain" $3.85 in San Francisco. If you prefer using cash for small purchases, make time to stop off at your in-network ATM so you don't rack up completely avoidable charges. You can also avoid overdraft fees and monthly fees. How? By checking out BankMobile!

Rule #7. Shop for great deals. Look for comparison shopping websites— Woot, BizRate, and Shopzilla, to name a mere three—or apps that do the same thing, like RedLaser, ShopAdvisor, and ShoppingScout. There are many others.

Your bank should be helping you comparison shop. It already has a lot of useful information about your annual salary, your repeat expenses, your lifestyle habits, and even your splurges. If you are in the market for, say, a smart TV, you should be able to take an in-store picture of the TV you like, send it off via smartphone to your bank, and wait for your bank —your financial *partner*—to tell you if you can afford to buy it. If the TV breaks your budget, your bank should be equipped to suggest a more affordable model at another store. This is a feature soon to be offered by BankMobile.

Rule #8. Pay your bills on time. If you do, you'll have a good credit rating. And if you've got a good credit rating, you will not only get approved for loans, you will pay lower rates on them. The same holds true for credit cards. If your credit is good, you can get a card that gives you two-to-five percent back on groceries, gas, and pharmacy purchases. A member of our team learned that long ago. That means that if you spend $1,000 a month, you'll get $600 back at the end of the year. Alternatively, if you currently carry a balance on your credit card, you can get a lower rate once you pay it off.

MANAGING YOUR LOANS AND DEBT

Nobody succeeds without doing some smart borrowing; not individuals, not businesses, not nations. How do you figure out how much you need to borrow—and how much you can afford to borrow?

Rule #1. Set a spending limit for yourself. Start out by looking at your weekly or monthly net paycheck; that is, the amount of income you have after all expenses including rent, utilities, taxes, and car payments have been deducted from your gross or "official" total income. What you have in front of you is a picture of how much you use to pay your bills and how much you have left beyond that to spend on other things.

Rule #2. Determine how much you can afford to spend at your discretion each week or month.

Rule #3. Set basic goals you want to achieve. Among these might be: Further your education, begin a pilot program for your business, plan a vacation, enlarge your wardrobe, move to a bigger apartment, buy a car, etc. Prioritize your goals because you won't be able to accomplish them all at the same time. Promise yourself that you won't deviate from your priorities. This is an important step if you are a gambler or an impulsive personality. If you train a laser focus on your priorities, you'll be able to stop yourself from overstepping your financial bounds.

Rule #4. Make sure to treat yourself to something you love *once in awhile*. If you really desire that latte, schedule it into your week, but only one time. Treating yourself once a week versus indulging every day is like watching one episode of *Game of Thrones* instead of binge-watching. If you watch just the one, you'll have time left to clean your house, throw together a simple meal for tomorrow's lunch, read a book or newspaper, exercise, or get together with friends or family. If you cut back on the number of lattes you drink in a week, you'll save money for all the other items on your priority list.

Rule #5. When borrowing money, do not overrate the value of minimum payments. Also, pay attention to the interest rate, fees and terms. Carefully look over the basic disclosures document. If the loan officer doesn't give you a copy, ask for it. You are entitled to see it.

Rule #6. Do your best to repay more than the minimum payment each month. You don't want to be paying off the car you bought in 2015 in 2020, by which time you might already have had some costly repairs done on it.

Rule #7. Avoid using your credit card if you have an outstanding balance on it. And remember that credit cards are for bigger purchases. For smaller purchases, such as gas and groceries, use a debit card.

Why not a credit card? Because it's a tool that makes you spend money you do not have. Then the credit card company sells that money back to you in the form of a minimum payment — and it gives the bank 18- to-25 percent interest beginning on the day you use it, and encourages you to make only minimum payments in order to spin out the debt to their own advantage. Do you really want to let them do that? Would you give your child a lump sum to spend as he sees fit and then tell him to pay you back one penny a month? A parent would never do that! Every penny you save on interest is money in your pocket.

Minimize impulse spending by thinking of your credit card as a debit card: Try your very best to pay off your balance in full.

Rule #8. Refinance your high-rate debt—especially if it has a long-term maturity—when rates are low. (Be aware of any punitive fees. Make sure you will not incur any prepayment penalties.) Definitely look into refinancing your car loan and mortgage, as well as your student debt.

Make your loan payments via direct payment from your paycheck. This way you'll never be late with an installment nd you'll never have to remember to write a check.

(While we're on the subject of college debt: Some very good changes to student debt repayment have come about in recent years, including legislation that caps monthly payments on certain loans, establishes fixed payments, and sets rates relative to your income level. How the federal government will absorb the debt is a matter beyond the purview of this book, but in short, you do not have to default on a student loan simply because you can't afford to pay it back at the moment.)

Rule #9. Ask your employer to help you reduce your student loan debt. If you are a valued employee, your manager might help you out with a performance-based bonus. These bonuses may come in the form of cash, flex time, or corporate perks—but you won't know if you can qualify because of your student debt unless you ask. No guarantees, but good companies tend to invest in their best employees.

PLANNING FOR MAJOR LIFE EVENTS

Rule #1. Invest in your career. If you are eighteen or older, it's time for you to take more responsibility for the upcoming events in your life. Even if you are fortunate enough to have parents who foot much of your college bill, you need to think about developing job and career skills—and you need to think about them as an investment, not an expense. We're not saying everybody should become a finance major or a computer programmer. We are saying you need to be entrepreneurial in your approach to your financial life, whether you're studying art history or quantum physics. If you want to be a fine arts painter, learn a computer graphics program so you can work part-time at a paying job. If you want to start a fashion business, set up exploratory conversations with industry people you admire. Find out what skills you need to survive and thrive and get them. There's no shame in taking a proactive approach to your career life. In fact, the more financially stable you are, the more free you will be—economically and psychologically—to concentrate your energies on the work you love.

Rule #2. Discuss money with your roommate, spouse, or partner. If he needs to have a smart TV in every room or if she needs a Caribbean vacation twice a year, you may find that you and your significant other are at financial crossroads. Having incompatible financial values nearly always spells marital trouble. You and your partner must be a single unit when it comes to saving and spending money.

Rule #3. Start saving for your married life—even before you meet your life partner. Realistically speaking, this may mean living with your family for a few months into your first job. Put that money into an account that you will not touch until you need a down payment for a house, a rental deposit, or money for a family car.

Incidentally, living at home after college should be a temporary arrangement. Under most circumstances, you do not want to be thirty years old and still sleeping in your childhood bed.

Rule #4. Start saving for your children's education as soon as they're born. This is the most important investment you will ever make. It is your duty as a parent to educate your kids and to encourage them to make their lives better than yours.

No one said it would be easy.

Tuition and fees at a typical public university in 2014-2015 were $9,139 per year. Room and board were $9,804. For an out-of-state student, tuition plus room and board clocked in at $32,762.

Tuition plus room and board at a private nonprofit university in 2014-2015 averaged $42,419.

If you have a baby today, she will be ready for college in eighteen years, when four years at a public university will cost an estimated $223,260, and four years at a private university $403,594. More specifically, Princeton will run you around $506,229; Rutgers $310,617. Gone are the days of a free city college education. From now on, educational betterment will not come cheap. Start saving today. *Anything. Something.*

Don't be like some of the people we run into who grumble about saving money for their children's college education. We know one father who complains that his daughter's college education is costing him so much that he wishes she would drop out. We know another father who resented his wife for having a fourth child; he didn't want to work an "extra" five years for the boy's college education. Bad! Bad! Bad! Bad! The lesson these dads are teaching their kids is that it is not important to succeed. If you're one of these dads—or moms—you are encouraging your children to mismanage their financial lives. You've got to cut that out.

One of the executives on our team met a father who gave his sons an education but advised his daughters to "marry rich." Our exec was so appalled that he ended his association with the guy. That's how seriously he takes education. So do we.

Rule #5. Save money for your retirement. When you're in your twenties, your sixties look far away. But if you stay healthy and you are lucky enough to live, your sixties will come all too soon! You don't want to spend your golden years eating Kibbles 'n Bits®!

If your employer offers you a 401(k), you must seriously give it a very close look. If you don't sign up for it, you are throwing away money. If your employer doesn't offer a 401(k), ask that one be set up. If this isn't possible, you have other retirement plan options. The Mighty Mini 401(k) plan, for example, is designed for employers with five or fewer employees. If an employer-sponsored retirement plan is out of the question, you can make contributions to either a traditional tax-deferred Individual Retirement Account, where you will pay taxes later; or a Roth IRA, where you pay taxes now. We recommend diversifying your retirement savings. Set up taxable *and* tax-free IRA accounts.

Recognize that income from Social Security can only supplement your retirement savings. You can't count on it to cover even your most basic everyday needs, and certainly not your rainy-day healthcare needs. The average Social Security check rings in at $15,228 a year. For a two-person household, the poverty line is $15,730. In 2011, the year for which we have the most recent statistics, nearly 3.6 million elderly people were living below the poverty line. That's 51 percent of seniors facing lower living standards upon retirement. Don't let this be you.

You'd be surprised by how little money you need to start investing in your retirement. Say, you're a teacher or a police officer at the beginning of your career. You are twenty-five and you plan on retiring at sixty-seven. Let's assume you make $26,667 a year and you contribute 10 percent of your gross pay to a retirement account. That's $2,666.67 per year. With an employer match, this number jumps to $4,000 per year. All told, you will have contributed $112,000 over the course of your working life. Based on an average seven percent return, your account balance at retirement age would be $1,244,281!

You could be a millionaire by the time you retire, even though you never made more than about $27,000 a year. We're not talking hocus- pocus here. This is how saving money works.

INVESTING YOUR MONEY

What I am about to advise you did not come from a book. I'm not a disciple of any investment guru. I didn't do any Google searches! I'm speaking from the heart and the head, based solely on my own experience as a banker over the last forty years.

Rule #1. Do not gamble. At least not until you have saved one year's worth of income. In that case, you can buy the risky stock or the investment property in a Florida swamp. Maybe you will strike it rich. But almost nobody does. Buying an investment property of any kind without researching it is a fool's game. If somebody has a tip for you based on his "gut," give him some Pepto-Bismol. Meanwhile, do your own research. If you're interested in a stock, don't just look at metrics, such as the price-earnings ratio. Read up on the company in books, newspapers, and on investment websites. Do you know what the company produces? Do you respect the management team? The more you know, the more you'll know how much to invest and for how long.

Never put your entire retirement fund into any single stock; there's no such thing as a sure thing. Spread your risk around by creating a diversified investment portfolio (index funds; mutual funds; individual stock; bonds; and liquid assets, i.e., cash).

If, after doing your due diligence, you decide to buy stock in a company, you need an entry and exit strategy. If you buy at, say, $18.50 per share, you might want to sell at $26 a share. You probably won't make a fortune on the sale (don't forget that you have to pay capital-gains tax), but you will have learned how to choose intelligently, wait patiently through the stock's ups and downs, and put your profit to good use.

In the interest of full disclosure, I confess that I have lost money by violating the very principle I now endorse. If you want to own stock, you have to remember the old investment adage: Bears make money. Bulls make money. Pigs go broke!

Rule #2. Take out your smartphone to study the best-performing Exchange Traded Funds (ETFs). These funds, which function as a basket of stocks, bonds, or commodities, are an easy way to diversify your investment portfolio. They are traded as a single unit close to their net asset value over the course of a trading day.

A reminder: You shouldn't buy stocks or bonds until you have saved at least six months' worth of your paycheck. Keep this money liquid; that is, in a bank account. You don't want to see the money you worked hard to save get wiped out by some unforeseen event like the 2008 financial crisis. This means that the more money you make, the more you need to save in that bank account.

Again, speaking from personal experience, I generally put 70 percent of my savings in stocks and 30 percent in deposits or bonds. I believe that this 70/30 investment strategy should be your rule of thumb up until ten years before your planned retirement. The closer you get to retirement, the more conservative you must become. You'll want cash with guaranteed income.

I have always stayed away from annuities, financial products designed by insurance companies to pay out regular income once you retire. The problem with annuities is that they carry absurdly high commission fees. In the case of a variable annuity, you can have your taxes deferred—but only upon the condition that your insurance company will charge you a bunch of fees *plus* a surrender charge when your annuity matures, *plus* a state premium tax, *plus* a ten percent penalty if you take your money out before you turn fifty-nine and a half. You could make more money by investing directly in a mutual funds IRA account. Long story short: If you decide you really want to buy an annuity, do your homework first.

SETTING MONEY ASIDE FOR TAXES

Never cheat on your taxes. But never pay more than you have to. You are not being virtuous by ceding control over your money to somebody else. Take advantage of all the deductions you're legally entitled to.

On average, Americans pay 28 percent of their income in taxes. In addition to taking all the deductions that are your due:

- Keep good records. Keep track of your bank and credit card statements and store receipts. Keep a spreadsheet of all your expenditures (gas, food, movies, phone, etc.).

- Do your own taxes. Hiring an accountant can cost upwards of 300 dollars. Learn how to use TurboTax. It'll walk you through the tax filing process and introduce you to the basics of tax preparation.

What we're trying to say is that life is not a straight line to financial success. Not for me. Not for Luvleen. Not for most people. If you're thinking, *It's easy for the Sidhus to talk, but they don't know how bad my financial troubles are*, we want to tell you that there is light at the end of the tunnel.

Whether you're a Millennial just starting out, or one of the 41 percent of traditional families struggling to make ends meet, or one of the 49 percent of non-traditional families living paycheck to paycheck, or one of the unbanked or underbanked millions, you can examine your spending habits and expenses to see where you can start saving money— even the tiniest amount to begin with. A big part of your personal savings plan depends on you educating yourself:

- About the role banks and other financial institutions play in your life. You'll see, sadly, that all too often they aren't on your side.

- About the importance of taking responsibility for your finances and for the future well-being of your family.

Gaining control over your financial health is a lot like managing your nutritional and physical health: Wherever you are right now is the only place you can start.

You are a human being. You can set a goal for yourself. Maybe you'll take two steps forward and one step back. That's a beginning. *That's nothing to be ashamed of.*

If you're reading our book, you are not starting at zero. You are already at 20 percent, which is the bonus advance that education gives you. If you keep learning about banks, savings, and investments, and take every opportunity to develop your career skills, you'll increase your chances of attaining financial peace of mind.

I want to encourage you to seek out opportunities to further your education. Nothing else has ever stood me in better stead in terms of my professional life and my personal life. Nothing.

I want you to know how committed I am to education as a way out and up. I was a twenty-four-year-old employee of Chemical Bank (today the financial backbone of J.P. Morgan Chase). I read about a corporate strategy course being taught at Dartmouth. I asked my manager if I could attend. He said the company couldn't afford to send me. I said fine, I'd pay for it myself.

The next day, my manager said he admired my resolve. He agreed to pay for my course.

When I got to Dartmouth, I was the only twenty-four year-old kid sitting in a room full of bank presidents. At the end of the day's session, I went out for some beers with these guys. The fellow I sat next to was president of Independence Bank Corp. We got to talking. He tried to tell me that corporate strategy is all about finance. Now, anyone who knows me knows I have my own views! I took issue with him. I said corporate strategy is all about execution through people. I said that if you hire the right people and you encourage them, you will come up with a corporate strategy they care about. I believed then, as I do now, that a mediocre plan superbly executed is so much better than a brilliant plan poorly executed.

Five days later, when I was already back at Chemical, I got a phone call from the president of Independence Bank Corp. He said he had a job opening for a chief operating officer. He wanted me to come in for an interview. Reader, he hired me!

By the time I was in my late twenties he had moved to Penn Savings Bank in Reading, Pennsylvania. He asked me to follow him. Over the next three years, we worked to transform Penn Savings into Sovereign Bank (today known as Santander Bank.) To my surprise, he announced one day that he was leaving the banking business to get a Ph.D. in psychology. I told him he was nuts!

Yet, because I was willing to pay my own way through the Dartmouth corporate strategy certificate, I ended up well placed to become the next president of Sovereign Bank.

Chutzpah. Derring-do. Intelligent risk-taking. You've got some of that inside you, too. Channel it into learning the skills that can help pave a path to a better life for yourself and the people who matter to you. Don't worry about being first or second or third. Wait for the less expensive train if it makes sense to do that. But just get on it. You have to keep moving forward.

We can help you do just that.

CHAPTER 7

It's Time to Dump Your Bank! Why BankMobile Is a Bank You Can Love

"NO, IT'S OKAY, CHASE. I'M RICH. YOU CAN CHARGE ME fees for deposits or pay me almost nothing for savings!"

"Well $#@& you very much, Huntington, for STILL not getting my debit card to me 3 weeks later. No Cyber Monday deals for me."

"I've invested too much time to just hang up."

"PNC . . . finding new ways to make your life difficult every day."

"I can't believe I have to give you my account number and name again for the *fifth* time. Don't you guys have systems that talk to each other?"

"Customers like me want a friction-free experience in banking, like a so-simple taxi service." (We did not make this up!)

All the touchy-feeling marketing in the world will never convince people that their own experience with banks is somehow atypical. These tweets from real people tell us that consumer banking in 2015 is what Baby Boomers used to call a "bad trip"— and it's a bad trip for millions of people. As much as we all have come to depend on mobile technologies to buy stuff, find love, hail taxicabs, and learn new things, the big banks can only respond to digital reality by doing what it's done for years: Hit us up with fees, pay almost no interest on savings, and make us feel as though they are doing us a favor. This is the case even though:

- **Banks closed some 2,464 branches between April 1, 2014 and March 31, 2015.** Closing branch offices should give banks an opportunity to reassess their fee-based business model. Yet they are still charging customers and increasing fees for overdrafts, unmet balance minimums, out-of-network ATM usage, account closures, and many other banking services that used to be free. If branch banking is on the wane, how does this even make sense?

For one thing, the past is still with us. Banks are trying to slash costs and capitalize on the shift to mobile banking, but they're hog-tied by legal costs that arose back in 2008, when they approved shoddy mortgages. In addition, interest rates remain low and banks can't make a profit on the difference between the interest they pay out on deposits and the amount they earn on loans.

"They don't want the deposits — and they don't want the branches," says Dick Bove, a banking analyst at Rafferty Capital.

As for the branches that persist: Some of them generate nearly one million dollars a year *per branch* in fees.

And here's something that will make your skin crawl: Fee revenue per branch is the highest in the nation at Fort Hood Bank. Bank customers, *mostly Americans serving in the U.S. armed forces*, have relatively limited assets. That means a chunk of branch revenue is most likely coming from overdraft and non-sufficient-fund fees. Clearly, this bank thinks it's okay to whack Americans who may end up making the ultimate sacrifice for their country.

- **Banks thought they would acquire a new revenue stream by lending to energy companies**. It really is true that nothing in life is certain but death and taxes. Oil prices sure aren't. In 2015, the price of crude oil tanked and now many energy companies can't service their huge debts. In short, bank revenue will not be coming from repayment of many of these loans.

- **Some banks think putting in more video screens and having lounges with sofas in branches will make more customers come and open checking accounts with fees.** How bananas is that!

We think it's safe to conclude that fees aren't going away any time soon, and many banks will not raise rates on savings even though the Fed has starting increasing interest rates.

Where does that leave you—the Millennial, GenXer, or Baby Boomer? You probably aren't keen on closing your checking account, because you've linked it with your automatic mortgage, phone, utility, cable, and insurance payments. And what's to say that if you open a new checking account you won't be hit with the same kinds of fees you thought you left behind?

We've been good about holding off on our pitch, but we need to make it now!

You have a choice.

It's BankMobile.

BankMobile is the first bank in the country to offer a complete fee free checking account, and it pays you higher interest rates on your savings.

✓ No fees to open a checking account or to close it.

✓ No fees to withdraw money or to deposit it.

✓ No fees to save money or to transfer it.

✓ No fees to use any of the 55,000 ATMs in our network.

✓ BankMobile never even charges a fee on an overdraft. We offer qualified customers a line of credit for rainy days and an automatic sweep from your savings account. If you drain your bank account, BankMobile will just close it. You won't suffer any additional penalty.

✓ No other mobile bank can make these claims.

We started BankMobile because we understand that banking today is an antiquated, frustrating experience for consumers. It is our mission to make banking affordable, effortless, and financially empowering. We want to be a bank you can love and trust! We understand the role that the current banking system has played in dimming the economic prospects for many people. We understand from the inside what you are going through and are determined to help you. Our client base includes:

- **Millennials** burdened with student debt, sometimes unable to find full-time work or unqualified, on the basis of income, to get a bank loan.

- **Middle-Class Americans**, living paycheck to paycheck, so cash-strapped that all too many rely on high-interest payday lenders to buy groceries, pay a utility bill, or make a mortgage payment.

- **Families** who want to manage their budgets well, who want mortgages, car loans, and help opening accounts for their children.

- **Underbanked and unbanked** low-income Americans who cannot afford a checking account and all the fees that go along with it.

- **Seniors** who are fed up with earning practically no interest on their savings, and who love the idea of free ATMs across the country.

It's hard to know what sources to believe when it comes to the state of the American economy. "Growth is likely to be robust in 2015—and will start to benefit ordinary families," *The Economist* trumpeted at the beginning of 2015. "U.S. consumers are feeling upbeat about the economy," largely because of a drop in gasoline prices, *The Wall Street Journal* wrote at the same time. Even a February 2015 jobs report, published by the Bureau of Labor Statistics, showed a decline in unemployment to 5.5 percent (8.7 million people) from 6.7 percent a year earlier. Definitely good news.

But these projections don't reveal what the news stories do.

First, wage growth has been stagnant. Average hourly earnings have risen less than two percent over the past year, a figure basically unchanged for the past five years. Indeed, the number of people in the labor force has declined, an indication that people who do not have a job or who have given up looking for one are still a factor in the economy.

Second, the number of new jobs slowed sharply for the second straight month in September 2015. Economists polled by Market-Watch, a Dow Jones website, were expecting a gain of 200,000 non-farm jobs, but the economy added only a seasonally adjusted 142,000 jobs. There is even a concern about a recession in 2016 and 2017.

The Pew Report talks about a paradoxical economic trend: Despite a "steadily increasing" national recovery, "most families feel vulnerable and stressed." Moreover, they "could not withstand a serious financial emergency." In a January 2015 study that looked at three components of family balance sheets—income, expenditures, and wealth—Pew concludes that the data reveal a "striking level of financial fragility":

- The typical worker had wage growth of 22 percent between 1979 and 1999, but only 2 percent from 1999-2009.
- In any given two-year period, nearly half of households experience an income gain or drop of more than 25 percent.
- Over the 22 years before the start of the economic downturn, household expenditures grew by 16 percent. Since 1990, the net increase in average annual household spending has been just 2 percent.

- At all income levels, households could not replace two months of income with liquid savings.

No single bank can wave a magic wand and change the state of family balance sheets from "precarious," as Pew calls them, to robust. No single bank can reverse social trends brought about by globalization, outsourcing, and the "disruptive" Internet economy.

What BankMobile can do, though, is recognize the severity of the overall financial situation among Millennials, Gen Xers, Baby Boomers, and the Silent Generation—i.e., everyone alive today—and take action to lighten the financial burden. We vow to:

- Let you do all you would do at a bank branch from the palm of your hand or your laptop or desktop.
- Help you sidestep the bank fees that have gotten a chokehold on Americans of nearly all financial and social conditions. (Why should Americans spend more per year on overdraft fees than what they spend on vegetables?)
- Make it possible to open an account in three to five minutes by simply snapping a photo of your driver's license and answering a few identity questions.
- Let you pay a bill just by taking a photo of it.
- Offer free access to 55,000 ATMs across the country.
- Bring you the kind of technology (with complete security) that can help you seamlessly manage your money.
- Offer you an interest rate on your savings that is at least 0.25 percent higher than the top four banks in the nation are offering at any time, so that you are rewarded for saving.

- Give you access to a personal banker who knows you well and is accessible via email, phone, or text chat anytime.
- Provide you with information—through our blogs, monthly newsletters, and free consultations with financial coaches—that can help you meet your financial goals and make more money.
- Eliminate branches so you aren't stuck financially supporting a dying, inefficient business model.

Did you know that the typical bank branch houses only about 1,500 retail checking accounts—but that banks spend about $1 million a year on personnel at each branch? What kind of economies of scale can you get from such low figures? Why should *you* pay for their bad business model?

In just its first year of existence, BankMobile attracted over 100,000 customers—with no branches. As we go to press, we are already serving about two million American customers and hope to add more than 500,000 new customers each year. You can join this revolution too, and help Americans save hundreds of millions of dollars in fees, and earn higher rates on their savings. Isn't this what you should expect from your bank that you love?

In our research, we found that some consumers already engage in regular online banking activities. None of them depends on coming into a branch office. Here are the things consumers have told us they want to be able to do from their smartphones:

- Check balances instantly on your smart phone or smart watch.
- Deposit funds.

- Withdraw money from any ATM in America.
- Transfer funds.
- Pay bills.
- Open accounts, joint or individual.
- See statements anytime.
- Get advice from a banker when they need it.
- Use Apple Pay or Samsung pay to make purchases.

BankMobile offers all this and a lot more.

We also learned that 20 percent of comments about banks and other financial institutions on Twitter and Facebook are downright hostile. Among the complaints most likely to prompt a consumer to leave a bank:

ACTION	Percentage of consumers
New or raised fee	48
Bad customer experience	21
Uncompetitive interest rates	11
Lack of up-to-date online features	6

BankMobile offers a completely fee free checking account, pays higher rates, and lets you use ATMs free all across America with any regular direct deposit. We provide a simple, easy-to-use app interface and the tools and education you need to manage your financial life.

Given the sluggish economy, and the preference among Millennials and tech-savvy GenXers and Baby Boomers for mobile banking, we had to ask ourselves, "If we could start from scratch, how would we build a bank that our customers would love?"

We determined that we would design a bank that works with the technology people use all the time: their smartphones, their tablets, and their laptops, and desktop computers.

That's exactly what we did.

To create BankMobile, we recruited a team with global experience in fields other than the banking industry. We spoke with the most successful technology companies and learned from them. We studied successful innovations in many industries. We kept our focus on customers' needs and aspirations. We may be avoiding physical branch offices, but we aren't neglecting the human touch: We're offering personal bankers for our retail and business customers twelve hours a day, seven days a week. That way, our customers can always communicate with someone who knows them. We can afford to do this because we embraced a banking philosophy that promotes growth through cost-efficiency *and* prudent, low-risk banking.

We are committed to continuous innovation and improvement. Our built-from-scratch bank can make guarantees that traditional brick-and-mortar banks can't. By the fourth quarter of 2015, BankMobile was paying a 0.75 percent Annual Percentage Yield (APY) on our savings accounts. (We guarantee a rate that is at least a quarter of a percent higher than the savings rate paid by the top four banks in the US.) We offer free access to 55,000 ATMs to all our customers, a credit line, and free consultations with a financial coach, as well as free access to every ATM in the United States for customers who directly deposit their paycheck.

No bank in America can match BankMobile.

We are inviting our customers to be our brand ambassadors by referring new customers. We're not being glib. If you're a college student, you can literally become a BankMobile brand ambassador by helping us spread the word about BankMobile in your college community. You'll be helping your classmates become financially empowered by encouraging them to sign up for our monthly financial education services. You'll make money and gain invaluable experience in running your own business.

By the end of 2016, we plan to have a similar program for all of our customers, so that they can all earn rewards or make money by spreading the word about BankMobile. We believe our best advertising is word of mouth.

We invite college and high school students to join us today. Like all good relationships, we'll gain a lot from working with each other. You'll help us broaden our customer base by giving out BankMobile swag and by using your superior social media skills to publicize our #LiveFreeBankFree message on Twitter, Facebook, Instagram, and other digital marketplaces. And we'll even help you gain marketing and business experience that you can put on your resume. Our top executives will even write you a reference! Now, *that's* something you can take to the bank.

Best of all, the top 10 college ambassadors will get a guaranteed summer internship with our BankMobile team in New York. We're accepting applications on our website, BankMobile.com.

We also want to build relationships with affinity groups—alumni organizations, unions, charities, religious institutions, and advocacy groups—much as USAA has solidified its relationship with U.S. veterans. We want to bring BankMobile to some 17.7 million union members and to employees of businesses of all sizes. We understand that these groups can benefit from a bank that offers them the most comprehensive and relevant products and services, and we think we can be extremely useful in this area.

Oh, yes. We are seriously committed to getting the word out so that *everybody* has access to an affordable, socially responsible way to bank.

How can we afford to be the first to offer a fee free banking experience for so many different kinds of people? For one thing, handling a transaction on a mobile phone costs 50 times less than the same transaction at a branch office, and 20 times less than the transaction on an online platform. A typical bank branch opens one net new checking account a week. By contrast, consumers by the thousands are joining BankMobile each week. That's how we are amassing the numbers of clients we need in order to make mobile banking profitable.

Most banks would say, "We also offer mobile apps." That's true. Yet they don't offer all of the benefits of BankMobile, and they're still charging you those obscene fees to boost their profitability and pay for all those branches. They don't provide a full suite of banking products and services, and they pay you practically nothing for the savings deposits you hold at their banks. They have minimal focus on personalization. And even though some claim to be fee-free, they have complicated small-print fee disclaimers.

Another thing our competitors don't do is ask *you* for advice. We have gotten many of our best ideas—taking a picture of your driver's license to open a BankMobile account, for example—from crowdsourced focus groups and social media cohorts. In March 2015, we rolled out a "Build Your Own Bank" contest on Facebook that invited people to submit their ideas (via video or image) for a product or feature they would implement if they were building their own bank. The winner, Stephanie Hall, received $5,000 for telling us her bank would combine her daily planner with her banking platform.

"Schedules usually revolve around our bank account, so why not put it in the same place?" she proposed in the *video* she sent us.

While creating a fee-free banking experience is at the heart of our business, we plan on debuting a lot of other features in coming years that no one—neither brick and mortar nor other mobile banks — has yet associated with mobile banking. Some of these features are predictable: Auto loans, credit cards, mortgages and certificates of deposit (CDs). Another will reward depositors with higher rates on checking accounts and discounts on purchases when they use our debit cards. We are building strategic partnerships so you can access all your financial needs through the BankMobile app. For example, we are partnering with other start-ups to offer free stock trading within the BankMobile app, for a seamless and effortless user experience.

We will also use data analytics to personalize your banking and shopping experiences, putting us on a path truly to become your Uber of banking. We believe you should be able to use your smartphone to search for a big-ticket item such as a car, look at other comparably priced cars, and get pre-approval for an auto loan even before you leave the auto lot or your car-shopping website. And one day soon, why not have awesome experiences shopping for homes and get pre-approved mortgage loans all on your smart phone?

Given the great number of Millennials eager to start their own businesses—and frustrated by the big banks' unwillingness to extend financing—we are instituting another transformational feature: the BankMobile Foundation. We are setting our own Shark Tank-like (although much friendlier!) board to review business plans that have great potential but insufficient funding, and we'll help make those ideas real. We cannot think of one other bank, mobile or branch-based, that plans on investing in people with the know-how to grow a business, hire employees, and contribute to the nation's wealth.

We launched our Foundation in 2015 by donating $5,000 to the *NJEA Frederick L. Hipp Foundation for Excellence in Education,* an organization dedicated to improving the learning environment in New Jersey public schools. BankMobile officially entered into a partnership with the New Jersey Education Association (NJEA) because of its commitment to financial literacy beginning in elementary school. We also provide annual scholarships for students who are on a mission to promote financial literacy in their communities.

We also believe that BankMobile can lead the way in biometric authentication. Who better than a financial institution, working with a biometrics services company, to help prevent identity theft and the loss of personal data? We want to work with biometrics developers experimenting with signature dynamics, eye scans, voice and facial recognition, and fingerprinting to make all of your financial and purchasing activities secure. Maybe the brick-and-mortar banks will get around to implementing biometric security someday, but when you're already using a smart device as your banking portal, it's not a stretch to add on biometric capabilities.

Have we made our case?

In many ways you've already decided. So much of your lives today are defined by Amazon, Facebook, Netflix, iTunes, LinkedIn, Twitter, WhatsApp, FitBit, GrubHub, Instagram, and Uber. Speed and access are the way you live. Traditional banking, with its fees and lack of contextual customer service, is the residue of an outmoded *lifestyle*. You don't live like that anymore.

What's the most important thing to look for in a bank? Is it its executive management team? Its vision for the future? Its strategic commitments to investment of revenues over cost-cutting? Its maximized use of software, social networks, and business apps to reduce operating expenses and insure customer satisfaction? Its strong capital base? Unquestionably, these factors underlie the success of any strong, successful, innovative bank. You could exhaust yourself researching banks to evaluate how they stack up regarding these factors...or you could make it easy on yourself and ask what bank already operates in tune with your lifestyle and focuses on all of the above.

You already know the answer to that one.

CHAPTER 8

The Future of Banking

HERE'S ONE LAST STORY OF HOW THINGS "USED TO BE"—
and where things are headed next.

Cheryl, 28, was a graduate student in economics. Before
she went off to the Toulouse School of Economics for a year,
Cheryl called her bank to ask if she had ATM privileges in France.
According to her service rep, she could use in-network ATMs
free of charge. Later on, Cheryl was surprised to see €3 – €4 per
transaction charges on her bank statement.

"A friend of mine in the program used the same bank," Cheryl
says. "She wasn't charged anything for using an ATM, but she [paid]
a fee every time she swiped her credit card." When Cheryl got back
to the U.S., she called her bank. "I didn't get anywhere with them
and I gave up," she says. If Cheryl, a budding economist, could get
taken advantage of by the current banking system, imagine how
many millions of other people have suffered, too.

But the headaches caused by out-of-touch, traditional financial institutions didn't end there. In 2010, Cheryl moved to China for a work-study assignment. She charged tuition and move-related expenses to her credit card. "One day, I look at my statement and I notice that the bank had reset my credit maximum from $14,000 to $1,000," Cheryl says. She was not permitted any further charges until she paid off the $1,000. A service rep at the bank told her that the new maximum was due to "market conditions."

In retrospect, Cheryl says, she should have been skeptical even before she left for France. "The service rep asked me if France was in Europe or if Europe was in France," she says.

Clearly, these banks are not working *for* the people—they're not even working *with* the people.

Say good riddance to banking as Cheryl knows it.

The interactions Cheryl had with her bank are going the way of Danish paper currency, which the government of Denmark is *considering doing away with*.[1] Even the service rep who didn't know much 'bout geography won't be much of a decisive factor in a financial services sector that's already been disrupted by two titanic forces: Millennials and digital technology.

We've already talked about Millennials and how they cut their teeth on technology. Now, as young adults, they use mobile technology to buy their airline tickets, navigate their travels, transfer their money, invest their savings, book their lodgings, hail their

---

[1] *Fortune* magazine, May 22, 2015: http://fortune.com/2015/05/22/Denmark-paper-money/

taxis, track their health, read their books, and check the weather anywhere in the world. The clunky technology experiences of their youth—waiting around for AOL to connect to the Internet, rewinding videocassette rentals, etc.—are faint memories. Amazon and other online providers are all part of their DNA. If we were social scientists instead of bankers, we might even argue that the "self-directedness" that defines these smartphone apps has engendered a self-directedness in millions of Millennials who prefer to do their own investment research, start their own charitable organizations, and create their own businesses. Research already bears out the independence and "personalization" mindset of the Millennial generation: More than two out of five affluent Millennials use Apple Pay, Google Wallet and Samsung Pay—the Near Field Communications (NFC) mobile payment platforms that are making cash and ATMs irrelevant to the way Millennials live. They are bypassing the banking system wherever they can.

This is a generation that is more and more impatient with the interactions that Cheryl, the 28-year-old economist, put up with five years ago as a visiting graduate student in France. These days, 69 percent of affluent Millennials say they are open to financial offerings from traditionally non-financial brands like T-Mobile, for instance. And why not? In a world of easy access to entertainment, education and retail services, why would Millennials tolerate credit-line restrictions, punitive fees on checking accounts, and uninformed customer service from a bank?

Bank products are currently a means to an end. Think about it; no one *likes* a mortgage, but they get one in order to purchase a house, which is the thing that gives them joy. Banks need to be more than just a means to sell products or services. BankMobile's goal is to provide value and add magical moments to people's lives—and, in the process, create loyal, lasting customers.

A bank could just sell mortgages, but imagine a bank that provides complete home-buying experiences. Just think of the possibilities inherent in a bank app that lets you see which homes in your area are available to purchase, that provides guidance as to whether they are in your price range, researches the estimated property taxes, extends you a mortgage in real time, and makes it possible for you to purchase the home straight from the app.

This kind of engaged user experience could apply to another of life's big purchases: a car. Banks could have a chance to not just sell auto loans but create a full car-buying experience with an app that allows customers to search for cars of their choice (complete with pictures and videos), and offers a simplistic user interface for securing a preapproved auto loan. The car is then delivered to the customer's home—with a bow on it! In the end, the customer has bought more than a car. They've created a memorable buying experience that they'll recommend to their friends, families, and loved ones.

#

Some people who use traditional bank help lines question the intelligence of the people who are trying to help them. Okay, that was a low blow! But seriously, some banks are now investing in companies that provide artificial intelligence to offer smart answers to complex financial questions. Another company offers a virtual assistant for banking customers that actually responds to voice prompts, a service Barclays Bank is also developing. Interest in robotics has increased among banks, who are concerned that Apple and Google, which possess of large amounts of customer data, could offer banking services of their own. The challenge banks face is to incorporate cutting-edge technology without appearing "faddish" and unpredictable, according to a *report* in *American Banker*.

The Brits are also ahead of the game when it comes to making it easier to switch banks. Open bank APIs or "application programming interfaces" allow British banking customers to switch banks quickly and easily, without the security risk involved in current methods of transferring data from one bank to another. The prospect is both "tantalizing and terrifying" for banks, *according to American Banker*. Banks must now find ways to make themselves indispensable to their customers, because it will be easier than ever for dissatisfied customers to up and leave.

Banks are also involving themselves in the Internet of Things. Let's say your refrigerator notices that you have run out of milk. It automatically orders a fresh carton from a nearby supermarket. Your bank communicates with your refrigerator—yes, really! —to handle the payment. Or your car might run low on oil, schedule a service appointment, and complete payment for you, via a connection with your bank, as you pull out of the garage.

Retirees will benefit from the latest in technology, too, but perhaps at a cost of privacy. Kitchen appliances can monitor cooking and eating habits and transmit that information to doctors. How do you hide the ice cream? Perhaps that kind of cognitive problem will help keep older people on their toes! And if they do have health issues, smart clothes will be able to detect activity levels and alert doctors to sudden changes. Banks will have to consider how else they can insert themselves into this suddenly transforming relationship between people and possessions.

Just as things are changing in homes, things are changing behind the scenes in banks, too. New technologies also obviate many banking tasks traditionally performed by humans, increasing speed and reducing the possibility of human error. Bank tellers, loan officers, mortgage brokers, and insurance underwriters, among others, are likely to see their roles diminish or even disappear as technology becomes more pervasive behind the scenes at banks. One Japanese bank now even employs a humanoid robot to greet and interact with customers. The robot speaks Japanese, Chinese, and English and studies facial expressions and behavior to provide appropriate responses to customer questions. The robot never takes a sick day!

The United States actually lags behind Europe when it comes to mobile banking. One such firm, Spain's Caixa Bank, reported that 92 percent of its deposits, withdrawals, and other transactions occur digitally or via ATMs. The vast majority of transactions that take place in bank branches are for commercial customers. In the Netherlands, only five percent of retail bank customers actually visit branches. American and British banks, by contrast, are too busy restoring their tarnished reputations to focus as intently on technology, which is a moving target and therefore hard to get a handle on.

Some American banks are so caught up in traditional ways of banking that the shift isn't just technological; it's cultural. BNY

Mellon actually has a contest to encourage employees of the 230-year-old company to think more about technology and less about "the way we've always done things around here." J.P. Morgan has joined forces with an industry upstart, OnDeck Capital, to approve small business loans on a scoring system in a matter of minutes instead of weeks, with funding taking place the next day.

The overall level of disruption for banks is unparalleled. The old world of 3-6-3 (pay three percent interest on deposits; loan the same money out at six percent; and be on the golf course by three) has gone the way of the bankbook, an old-school paper book used to record transactions on a deposit account. For both, there are simply better alternatives. Banks are getting the picture that they have to reinvent themselves and will no longer be able to get away with the self-serving highhandedness that has traditionally been their hallmark of "customer service."

We said at the outset of this book that banks view their customers as piñatas, from which they may extract fees practically at will. Going forward, startups like BankMobile and established tech companies like Google, Apple, and Microsoft will turn the tables and treat the traditional banking industry as a piñata: an aging, out-of-touch industry ripe for creative destruction. And the real winners will be the customers, who will laugh all the way to their virtual new banks!

#

The loose cannon in this strange new world of mobile technology is fintech—companies that develop digital technologies to make financial systems more efficient, cheaper, and easier to use.

Fintech developers (there were over 5,000-6,000 in 2015 alone) are creating apps and systems under a big tent that includes:

- Asset management (Betterment, WealthFront, Robinhood, Acorns)
- Thematic investing (Motif)
- Peer-to-peer lending (Lending Club, Prosper)
- Crowdfunding (Indiegogo, Kickstarter)
- Payments (Square Cash, Paypal, nTrust, Venmo, Stripe, Braintree)
- Payroll (Even, ActiveHours, FlexWage, PayActiv)
- Credit scoring (Credit.com, Credit Karma)
- Small-business lending (Kabbage; OnDeck, CAN Capital)
- Digital currency (CoinBase, Circle, Bitcoin, OpenCoin)
- International Currency Transfers (Transferwise)
- Exchanges (SecondMarket)
- Working capital management (Tesorio)
- Cyber security (Vasco, Experian, LexisNexis)
- Distributed ledgers (Bitcoin, Ethereum)

As we publish this book, we see that many banks provide vanilla online and mobile access to checking accounts. When it comes to developing the kind of technology-based products and services as represented by our list above, though, banks are asleep at the wheel.

With the proliferation of fintech companies across the financial services spectrum, banks have to ask themselves if fintech is a threat to their own business model. If it is, banks need to decide if they are going to compete against the upstarts or acquire them. If banks opt for acquisition, will they be able to embrace twenty-first century innovation while also browbeating their customers with overdraft charges and other punitive fees? Can you be a dinosaur and a unicorn—a billion-dollar tech start-up—at the same time?

We think not, because at the heart of fintech innovation is the push for efficiency. Seamlessness. Customer satisfaction. Cost savings. We're not saying banks are doomed; just that they're in danger of hoisting themselves on their own petard and losing millions of customers to better ways of doing things. They're in danger of hanging themselves out to dry in a technology environment that, amazingly, isn't only about competition but about making the connected economy bigger, more all-encompassing, and more efficient than it is today.

#

The fintech that inevitably will catapult banks into an innovation mindset is the distributed ledger platform.

A distributed ledger, or blockchain, is a database stored in multiple computers in the same location or dispersed over a network of interconnected computers. Its purpose: to house an ever-expanding, ever-changing list of data records and transactions. Theoretically, at least, the distributed nature of the technology, as well as the constant "shape shifting" of the data, should keep would-be hackers at bay.

Bitcoin is a digital peer-to-peer cryptocurrency whereby investors can acquire virtual "coins" and make transactions that are recorded on a distributed ledger. The Bitcoin blockchain insures that once a transaction has been recorded, the transaction can't be changed. A lot of financial services companies have adopted or are on the verge of adopting blockchain technology. The NASDAQ exchange plans on using it to record trades in privately held companies. Excited by the possibility of protecting their ledgers against cyber-terrorists and money launderers, UBS, Goldman Sachs, J.P. Morgan, and twenty-two other banks have invested in a blockchain startup called R3 CEV that's developing a standardized architecture for private ledgers. In a 2014 research paper, the venerable old Bank of England wrote that distributed ledgers represent a "significant innovation" with "far-reaching implications" for the finance industry. For banks, a distributed ledger that operates by means of intricate, tamper-proof computerized "supply paths" — and not through a "trusted third party" central bank—is probably the most far-reaching implication of all.

Imagine being replaced by a bunch of computers ("nodes" in Bitcoin parlance) that mathematically agree on how to update the blockchain every time somebody transfers digital currency from one person to another!

Bitcoin poses other challenges to the banking community. The attraction of Bitcoin is privacy; transactions are practically untraceable. This is a problem for law enforcement, because terrorists could use Bitcoin to transfer funds without anyone knowing. Bitcoin also presents a problem for banks, who are legally bound to know their customers, to avoid the possibility of money laundering or other financial crimes. The privacy Bitcoin offers keeps banks from fulfilling that legal requirement.

In any event, blockchain technology is going to transform more than currency storage and payment processes. By adding a small amount of information to a Bitcoin transaction, you'll be able to transfer *any* asset, from land titles to automobiles, to anyone. Embedded in the ledger, that information indelibly confirms your ownership of any given item or service.

Thanks in large part to a startup called Ethereum, distributed ledgers will also let contracts and invoices "execute" themselves. But as 21-year-old co-inventor Vitalik Buterin says, offering up these smart contracts isn't what makes Ethereum special. What's unique, he says, is the open-source, democratic, corruption-free nature of distributed ledger technology: The scripting language actually lets anybody code a specific contract through a mechanism called—simply—contracts. "A contract is like an autonomous agent that runs a certain piece of code every time a transaction is sent to it, and this code can modify the contract's internal data storage or send transactions," he writes. "Advanced contracts can even modify their own code."

(We should mention that Buterin and his three co-inventors raised $18 million to start Ethereum. Using Bitcoin technology, they spent exactly $350 in transaction fees. Talk about starting a company in your garage!)

This boy wonder goes on to predict that Ethereum contracts will let users design crop insurance, savings wallets with withdrawal limits, peer-to-peer gambling, decentralized Dropbox- and eBay-style data storage, and decentralized autonomous organizations.

Should we run that one by you again?

Decentralized autonomous organizations.

DAOs are basically corporations run "without any human involvement under the control of an incorruptible set of business rules," as Dan Larimer, the inventor of another cryptocurrency, put it. You become a stakeholder in a DAO by buying stock in the company or by voluntarily participating in tasks. You can add value toward a common goal by collaborating with other stakeholders. As an owner of stock, you may be entitled to a share of the profits. The DAO gains critical mass as its operations become distributed and decentralized across a wider net. In the end, various smart programs, like contracts insure the DAO's autonomous sustainability.

The very notion of distributed ledgers has the potential to transform what we think of as a company. Will such organizations have—or need—leaders? With the existence of a trustworthy computing system, will they require real-world trusted third parties? What will be the significance of a brick-and-mortar branch network in a business model that makes branch-generated fees obsolete?

#

We began this chapter by talking about the self-directedness of the Millennial generation. What's more self-directed than a distributed ledger whose goal is an autonomously run computing system that lets organizations and countries (and you) transfer and receive money, goods, and services at a dramatically low cost, and lets you define the precise nature of the exchange?

What really matters is the role that self-directed systems like Bitcoin or Ethereum can have in changing the world for the better.

The power of distributed ledgers to improve the lives of millions, perhaps billions, of people around the world makes us think of some comments a notable banking analyst made about the underbanked. "There's no such thing," he says. "Just because someone chooses to use payday lending or check cashing services doesn't make them underserved." About the three billion unbanked people around the world, he says, "Banks and credit unions should focus their energies on the segments of customers and prospects that they can make money from. There's a reason the unbanked are unbanked—there's no money in serving them."

How's that sit with you?

Yeah, we thought so. We feel the same way.

Here's the thing about distributed ledgers: They can level the playing field so that it's not just us four billion first-worlders that stand to benefit from technology.

What would our planet be like if people in Afghanistan, Sudan, Brazil, and other unbanked regions of the world had access to financial services and the sort of documentation you need to prove that you own a piece of land or the house you're living in? What if the unbanked could verify that they had the skills to install clean-water systems, sell their family's homegrown vegetables, or teach children how to read, write, and cipher? What if they had a way to insure their homes, cars, bicycles, pedicabs, sewing machines, and jewelry? What if they didn't have to rely on taking out loans from family and friends, or pay a 15 percent remittance fee every time they received money from a relative living abroad? What if they could depend on a written contract instead of a verbal handshake? And what if they had access to the Internet?

What if the unbanked had a chance at living more or less the way we do?

They wouldn't be contributing to the $540 billion global remittance industry every time a relative wired them money. They wouldn't be paying 35 percent interest on a loan. They wouldn't be terrified at the prospect of getting sick, being robbed, or dying, because they could protect themselves and their families against disaster by buying insurance. They wouldn't have quite so much trouble proving that the house they've lived in for decades belongs to them.

The unbanked currently own something like $10 trillion worth of property and assets that they have no objective way of verifying that they own them. Ten trillion dollars. Maybe it's time that banks and credit unions started focusing their energies on the unbanked.

The technology that will help the global unbanked mine that money is the same technology that undergirds Bitcoin: a censorship-resistant blockchain, low-cost decentralized transaction systems, and inexpensive peer-to-peer contracts.

Technology can offer the unbanked the same thing we have: a documented reputation that paves the way to an education, a driver's license, a house of our own, and financial services.

We're optimists! And while we know that the most brilliant technology can't cure humankind of its aggressions, we believe it nevertheless has the power to whittle away at poverty, illiteracy, and infant mortality.

#

Meanwhile, you can count on the bank branch office to fade away. It's not just that 40 percent of Millennials would consider banking without a branch, or that 68 million Americans are under-banked or unbanked, or that by 2020 at least 66 percent of the global population will be online. The reality is that with each passing month, the bank branch is increasingly too expensive to keep up. How expensive? Well, 70 percent of the unbanked in Africa would have to spend their *entire life savings* if they wanted to set foot in the nearest branch office.

For a while, you'll still see banks that cannot accept the global embrace of smartphone banking. Seventy-five thousand branches will dot the banking landscape over the next three to five years, but these holdouts will be like Dennis on the TV series *30 Rock*—the last living beeper salesman in a world of smartphones.

Listen closely: That's the thunderous hoof-beat of fintech unicorns! Thirty-six now exist around the world, and another 32 are on their way to a unicorn valuation. They will join the 8,000 fintech startups already designing alternatives to the obsolescing branch model.

Like Domino's Pizza, which bills itself as a tech company, the biggest, most customer-friendly banks will be technology or even software companies. And when we say technology, we don't mean that the branch will become an Apple Store lookalike. It makes sense for Apple to invite customers into a store where they can touch the different kinds of Apple Watches or iPads. But you don't even have to get out of bed to try out a phone app.

153

A perfect storm of social media, cloud computing, and big data analytics is doing for banking what personalized medicine is doing for healthcare. Innovative banks will create analytical models that will drive revenue, control costs, mitigate risk—and uniquely serve their individual and small business customers. By using data from their own records and combining it with data from, say, Facebook or Twitter, banks can get a 360-degree view of their customers' behavior that will let them anticipate what product is on the next-to-buy list. The benefit to the customer: You'll be offered a product targeted to your personal or business financial needs, not some product bank management is pushing on you for their benefit.

A bank that understands the importance of listening to its customers will use data analytics to take customer feedback seriously. BBVA, for example, a global group that offers its 47 million individual and corporate customers a range of financial and non-financial products and services, is using an analytical model to address negative customer feedback. BBVA has already worked to improve its processes and renew its commitment to corporate social responsibility programs. This is a win-win for the bank and its customers.

Another smart user of data analytics, MoneyGram International, has prevented more than $200 million in fraud and money laundering by using software that makes correlations among different data fields. Based on weightings and rules, the program sends out alerts reviewed by MoneyGram analysts. In one case, an elderly woman came to a MoneyGram kiosk to send $2,500 to her grandson. Nothing immediately suspicious there — and yet the analysts got an alert indicating that something wasn't right. They denied the transaction. The woman was furious. She threatened to take her business elsewhere. But three days later, she called MoneyGram to say that the person who asked her for $2,500 was a con artist, not her grandson. In tears, she thanked MoneyGram for its due diligence.

Banks can use comparable data analytics models that combine customer behavior, geolocation, transaction history, and search engine queries to offer their customers financial advice and product offers. After all, banks are better equipped than any other retailer to evaluate what people buy and how much they spend in a typical day, week, year, or decade. Banks are sitting on a vastly underutilized trove of data that could serve as the basis for a marketplace of financial solutions. Banks should create—or encourage third parties to create—application programming interfaces (APIs) that make it easy for customers to port their transaction history from one institution to another, or to lend their money out to the highest FDIC-insured institutional bidder. An innovative bank might even offer an app that links the Internet of Things—your interconnected thermostat, refrigerator, bathroom scale, treadmill, car, and parking garage, for example—with a payment system API. The advantage for customers is clear: They gain more control over their own deposits and withdrawals— over their own money.

But what's the advantage for the banks? Banks could become a marketplace for all kinds of transactional apps. They would get a cut every time a customer used the app or a developer used the banks' APIs. Nothing farfetched there. The idea is already gaining traction in Europe.

#

Automation—the future for a host of routine banking transactions—has already made inroads into all kinds of white-collar work.

The discovery process in large lawsuits, for example, which once relied on newbie lawyers to sift through volumes of documents, now uses syntactic analysis and keyword recognition programs for the task. Logistics giant FedEx, too, is using fewer and fewer human beings to deliver packages and other business-related cargo. It plans on replacing its in-air pilots with drone-operated flights by 2020. In some cases, teachers are being replaced with math-instructing robots.

Physicians aren't immune to being replaced by machines either: Johnson & Johnson's sedation system automates delivery of low-level anesthesia during colonoscopies for much less money than an anesthesiologist. And thanks to massive amounts of data, IBM's Watson is offering up a more accurate diagnosis rate for lung cancers than humans—90 percent versus 50 percent in some tests.

Indeed, automated processes and big data analytics should immediately command the banks' attention. Software programs are displacing the economists and number-crunchers who until recently produced corporate earnings reports, marketing messages, and ad placements.

You can run but you cannot hide.

Some financial firms are turning to automated services, big data, and predictive analytics to gain insight into customer behavior. Automated financial advisor SigFig, for example, asks its online users to input their age, household income, percentage of savings from income, liquid assets, and risk tolerance. Within *seconds*, SigFig builds an investment plan based on those metrics. The primary users of "robo-advisors" will be younger Millenials, whose investment needs initially may not be that complex.

Banks have tons of customer data. What they need now is the fire in the belly to beat out Google, Apple, Facebook, and Amazon—non-bank competitors that are treading into banking territory with automated mobile payment offerings and financial services. Just take a look at the potential of non-bank tech companies to combine big data insights with fintech systems:

- Google+ members who interacted socially with any of Google's services in October 2013 total 540 million, up from 390 million earlier the same year.

- As of late 2013, Apple boasted 800 million iTunes account holders, most of whom had credit cards on file.

- Facebook passed 1.9 billion monthly active users in late 2013 and has an e-money license to offer financial services in Europe.

- Amazon has "only" 41.3 million unique buyers in the US, but they spend more on Amazon products than they do on, say, iTunes. Amazon has detailed credit card info from their clients.

Right now, the main thing that cools the financial jets of these four tech titans is tough regulation. "Tech companies are very reluctant to enter the banking game because of the regulatory regime," says PricewaterhouseCooper's Dave Hoffman. "In the end, deposit insurance is an important element of the trust factor that banks do have."

We're pretty sure, though, that the "trust factor" alone won't defang the Google-Apple-Facebook-Amazon nexus. These guys are going gangbusters to develop digital technologies that will deliver better or entirely new ways of meeting customer needs, even if they have to bypass regulation and redefine the banking industry in the process.

#

Bankers cannot live and breathe money all day long without wondering why life isn't better than it is—and not just for the three billion unbanked in the world, but for Cheryl, the Millennial economist who started us off with her tales of banking absurdities. A banking system that is fair empowers every single one of us to go after what we want in life: a business, a house, a healthcare plan, an education, a trek in the Andes. It won't hold onto systems designed for an earlier era, and then trip us up at every turn just because the world has moved on and it hasn't.

Human beings never seem to tire of talking about the need for revolution or for a new world order. We're two people in the financial services world who are saying that the power to improve our lives and the lives of others is already within reach.

Join us as we use incredible technologies like mobile and—one day—distributed ledgers to live financially empowering lives. Because once we get our own house in order, we can look beyond our good fortune to help others get theirs in order, too.